Praise for Oblivion

'As an account of the love between a son and his father it is
most moving. But it is also a clear-sighted exploration of
the terrible sickness that afflicted Colombia in the 1980s,
some pages so painful that one flinches from reading them.
In all, it is a tragic and unforgettable history.'
JOHN COETZEE

'This searing memoir written with love and blood is an act
of courage in its own right.'
New York Times

'Not only is it a beautiful and profoundly moving work, not
only is it a necessary lesson on current themes such as
civic education and the relation between personal and
historical memory, but it is also an irreplaceable testimony
of the struggle for democracy and tolerance in countries
that are so near and dear to us.'
FERNANDO SAVATRE, *El País*

'*Oblivion* is an admirable effort at speaking the unspeakable,
at verbalizing the pain accumulated over decades; it's been
years since I read such a powerful meditation on loss.
Abad's desire to explore the echoes of memory with
meticulous care, to touch the wound of the past through
lucid prose, is an act of valor.'
ILAN STAVANS, *San Francisco Chronicle*

'A loving and sentimental memoir that is both moving and
informative.'
Publishers Weekly

HÉCTOR ABAD was born in Medellín, Colombia, in 1958, where he studied medicine, philosophy, and journalism. He is one of Colombia's most beloved authors, and a translator of Umberto Eco. He moved to Italy after being expelled from university for criticizing the pope, and returned a second time in '87, after his father was murdered and he himself began to receive death threats. He has written various books, among which is his internationally acclaimed novel *The Farm*. The Spanish edition of *Oblivion* has sold over 250,000 copies. Abad currently lives in Colombia.

ANNE MCLEAN has translated works by Javier Cercas, Evelio Rosero, Ignacio Martínez de Pisón, Carmen Martín Gaite, Enrique Vila-Matas, and Julio Cortázar. Twice-winner of both the Independent Foreign Fiction Prize and the Premio Valle-Inclán, McLean won the IMPAC Dublin Literary Award in 2014 with Juan Gabriel Vázquez, and she was awarded a *Cruz de Oficial* for Civil Merit in 2012 in recognition of her contribution to making Spanish literature known to a wider public.

ROSALIND HARVEY is an acclaimed literary translator of contemporary Hispanic writing. She has worked on books by authors such as Enrique Vila-Matas, Elvira Navarro, and Guadalupe Nettel. Her translation of Juan Pablo Villalobos's debut novel, *Down the Rabbit Hole*, was shortlisted for the Guardian First Book Award, the Oxford-Weidenfeld Prize, and the PEN translation prize. Her latest translation is Nettel's *After the Winter*, with MacLehose Press/Coffee House Press.

OBLIVION

A MEMOIR

HÉCTOR ABAD

OBLIVION

A MEMOIR

Translated from the Spanish by
Rosalind Harvey & Anne McLean

WORLD EDITIONS
New York, London, Amsterdam

Published in the UK in 2019 by World Editions Ltd., London

World Editions
New York/London/Amsterdam

Printed by Mullervisual/Mart. Spruijt, Amsterdam, Netherlands

British Library Cataloguing-in-Publication Data
A catalogue record for this book is available on request from the British Library.

ISBN 978-1-912987-00-9

First published as *El olvido que seremos* in Spain in 2006 by Editorial Planeta Colombiana, S.A.

Twitter: @WorldEdBooks
Facebook: WorldEditionsInternationalPublishing
www.worldeditions.org

Book Club Discussion Guides are available on our website.

For Alberto Aguirre and Carlos Gaviria,
survivors

And for the sake of remembering
I wear my father's face over mine.

Yehuda Amichai

1

In the house lived ten women, one boy and a man. The women were Tatá, who had been my grandmother's nanny and was almost a hundred years old, partially deaf and practically blind; two girls who did the cooking and cleaning—Emma and Teresa—my five sisters: Maryluz, Clara, Eva, Marta and Sol; my mother and a nun. The boy, me, loved the man, his father, above all things. He loved him more than God. One day I had to choose between God and my dad, and I chose my dad. It was the first theological disagreement of my life and I had it with Sister Josefa, the nun who looked after Sol and me, the two youngest. If I close my eyes I can still hear her harsh, gruff voice clashing with my childish one. It was a bright morning and we were out in the sun on the patio, watching the hummingbirds doing their rounds of the flowers. Out of the blue, the Sister said to me:

'Your father is going to go to hell.'

'Why?' I asked.

'Because he doesn't go to Mass.'

'What about me?'

'You're going to go to heaven, because you pray with me every night.'

In the evenings, while she got undressed behind the folding screen with the embroidered unicorns, we said Hail Marys and the Lord's Prayer. At the end, before going to sleep we recited the Creed: 'I believe in God, the Father Almighty, Creator of Heaven and Earth, and of all things visible and invisible ...' She took off her habit behind the screen so we wouldn't see her hair; she'd warned us that seeing a nun's hair was a mortal sin. I, who understand things well, but slowly, had spent the whole day imagining myself in heaven without my father (I was leaning out a window in paradise and I could see him down below, pleading for help as he burned in the flames of hell), and that night, when she began to recite the prayers from behind the unicorn screen, I said:

'I'm not going to pray anymore.'

'Oh, no?' she challenged me.

'No. I don't want to go to heaven anymore. I don't like heaven if my daddy's not going to be there. I'd rather go to hell with him.'

Sister Josefa leaned around the screen (it was the only time we saw her without her veil, that is, the only time we committed the mortal sin of seeing her messy, unattractive hair) and shouted: 'Hush!' Then she crossed herself.

I loved my father with a love I didn't feel again until my own children were born. When I had them I recognized it, because it is an equally intense love, although different, and in a certain sense its opposite. I felt that nothing could happen to me if I was with my father. And

I feel that nothing can happen to my children if they are with me. That is, I know that I would give up my own life, without a moment's hesitation, to defend my children. And I know my father would have given his life, without a moment's hesitation, to defend me. As a child the most unbearable idea was that my father might die, and so I resolved to throw myself into the River Medellín if he did. Likewise, today I fear the death of one of my children much more than my own. All this is a very primitive, ancestral thing, which one feels in the deepest depths of consciousness, in a place that precedes thought. It is something one does not think, but which simply is, without any mitigating factors; something one knows not with the head but with the guts.

I loved my father with an animal love. I liked his smell and also the memory of his smell on the bed when he was away on a trip. I would beg the maids and my mother not to change the sheets or the pillowcase. I liked his voice, I liked his hands, his immaculate clothes and the meticulous cleanliness of his body. I felt for my father the same way my friends said they felt about their mothers. When I was afraid during the night, I would go to his bed and he would always make space for me at his side to lie down. He never said no to me. My mother protested—she said he was spoiling me—but my father moved over to the edge of the mattress and let me stay. I inhaled my father's scent, put my arm around him, stuck my thumb in my mouth, and slept soundly until the sound of horses' hoofs and the jangling of the milk cart announced the dawn.

2

My father let me do anything I wanted. Perhaps *anything* is an exaggeration. I couldn't do disgusting things like pick my nose or eat dirt; I couldn't hit my little sister ('not even with a rose petal'); I couldn't go out without telling someone I was going out, or cross the road without looking both ways. I had to be more respectful to Emma and Teresa (or any of the other maids we had in those years: Mariela, Rosa, Margarita) than to any guest or relative; I had to bathe every day, wash my hands before and brush my teeth after eating, and keep my fingernails clean ... But I was meek, and learned these basic things very quickly. By *anything* I mean that I could take, for example, his books or records whenever I wished, and touch his things (his shaving brush, handkerchiefs, bottle of aftershave, record player, typewriter, pen) without asking permission. I didn't have to ask for money either. He put it like this:

'Everything I have is yours. There's my wallet, take what you need.'

And there it was, always, in the back pocket of his trousers. I took my father's wallet out and counted the money he had. I never knew whether to take a peso, two pesos or five pesos. I'd think about it for a moment and decide not to take anything. My mother had warned us often:

'Niñas!'

My mother always called us *niñas* because the girls were a clear majority so therefore the grammatical rule (one man among a thousand women turns the whole group masculine) didn't count for her.

'Niñas! Professors are paid very badly in this country, they earn almost nothing. Don't take advantage of your father because he's silly and gives you whatever you want. He can't help himself.'

I knew that my father would let me take all the money in his wallet. Sometimes, when it was at its fullest, at the beginning of the month, I'd take out a twenty-peso note while my father was having his siesta and take it to my room. I'd play with it for a while, knowing it was mine, and fantasize about buying things (a bicycle, a football, an electric car set, a microscope, a telescope, a horse) as if I'd won the lottery. But I would always put it back later. There was hardly ever very much money, and sometimes, at the end of the month, none at all. We weren't rich, although it seemed like we were because we had a place in the country, a car, domestics and even a resident nun. When we asked my mother if we were rich or poor, she always answered the same way: 'Niñas, we are neither one nor the other. We're comfortable.' My father often gave me money without my asking, and then I had no qualms in accepting it.

My confusion about gender, grammatical and other-wise, displayed itself the first time I managed to comb my own hair. Having neatly parted it on the right (the wrong side for a boy), I asked my sisters, referring to myself with a feminine diminutive:

'*Quedé bien peinadita?* Does my hair look pretty?'

I can still hear the chorus of giggles from all five girls ringing in my ears. I've never combed my hair since.

According to my mother, and she's right, my father was incapable of understanding household finances. Against her husband's wishes, she had gone to work in a little office downtown: his professor's salary never stretched to the end of the month and, since my father had no concept of saving, there were no reserves to fall back on. When the utility bills arrived, or when my mother told him they had to pay the builder who'd repaired the leaky roof, or the electrician who'd fixed the short circuit, my father would get in a bad mood and shut himself up in his study to calm down, reading or listening to classical music at full volume. He was generally the one who had hired the builders, but he always forgot to ask beforehand how much they would charge for their work, so they ended up charging whatever they liked. If my mother arranged for repairs, she would get a couple of quotes, do some haggling, and as a result there were never any surprises when the job was done.

My father never had enough money because he always gave or lent money to anyone who asked—relatives, acquaintances, strangers, beggars. The students at the university took advantage of him. So did the caretaker of the farm, Don Dionisio, a brazen Yugoslav who made my father give him advances on future apples, pears and Mediterranean figs that never showed up in our orchards. In the end Dionisio bought some land of his own with these advances, and used it to set up a business on the side, selling strawberries and garden vegetables he'd propagated from our stock, and doing quite well for himself. Then my father hired our maid Teresa's parents, Don Feliciano and Doña Rosa, to be the caretakers, as they'd been starving to death up in Amalfi, a village in the northeast. Unfortunately Don Feliciano, almost eighty years old and racked by arthritis, was incapable of looking after the crops, so within six months Don Dionisio's vegetables and strawberries had gone to ruin and the farm was choked with weeds. But of course we couldn't send Doña Rosa and Don Feliciano back to Amalfi to starve to death for the sake of a few spoiled vegetables: we'd have to wait for them to die of old age. And in the end that's what happened, whereupon Edilso and Belén moved in as the new caretakers. Thirty years later they are still there, under a very strange contract of my father's invention: we supply the land, they look after the cows and all the milk is theirs to keep or sell.

I knew that his students frequently asked him to lend them money because I often accompanied him to the university, and his office resembled a place of pilgrimage, with students lined up outside the door. It's true that some wanted to discuss academic or personal matters, but most were there to ask for loans. Whenever I was there, I'd see my father take out his wallet several times to hand over bills that would never be returned. Consequently there was always a swarm of scroungers around him.

'Poor kids,' he'd say, 'they can't even afford lunch; and it's impossible to study when you're hungry.'

3

Before I started kindergarten, I didn't like having to stay at home every day with Sol and the nun. When I tired of my solitary little boy's games (fantasies on the floor with castles and soldiers), the most entertaining thing Sister Josefa could think of, apart from praying, was to watch the hummingbirds sipping at the flowers on the patio. Or sometimes we went for a stroll around the neighbourhood, Sister Josefa pushing my sleeping sister in the buggy, while I rode on the bars at the back when I got tired of walking.

This daily routine bored me, so I would ask my father to take me along to his office, in the Department of Public Health and Preventative Medicine at the Faculty of Medicine, next door to Saint Vincent de Paul Hospital. If he was too busy to have me with him that morning, he would at least take me for a drive around the block. I'd sit on his knees and steer, while he kept an eye on me. His car was a big, old, noisy, pale blue Plymouth, an automatic, that started to overheat and smoke under the bonnet at the very sight of the first slope. But whenever he could, at least once a week, my father did take me to the university. On the way in we went past the amphitheatre where anatomy classes were taught, and I would beg him to show me the cadavers. He would always answer: 'No, not yet.' We had the same exchange every week:

'Daddy, I want to see a dead person.'

'No, not yet.'

Once, when he knew there wasn't a class, or a corpse, we did go inside the amphitheatre, which was very old; the kind with stands all around so students could get a good view of the dissection. In the centre of the room was a marble slab for the protagonist of the class, just like in the Rembrandt painting. That day the amphitheatre was empty of cadavers, students and anatomy professors. However, in this emptiness there persisted a smell of death, like an impalpable ghostly presence, that made me aware, in that very moment, of my heart beating in my chest.

While my father was teaching, I would sit at his desk and wait for him, drawing pictures or pretending to write, tapping at the typewriter the way he did, with the index finger of each hand. From the distance, Gilma Eusse, the secretary, watched me, smiling mischievously —I don't know why. She had a framed wedding photo of herself in a bridal gown, marrying my father. I asked over and over again why she had married my father, and she would explain, smiling, that it had been a wedding by proxy, to a Mexican man named Iván Restrepo, and that my father had merely represented him in the church. While she told me of this incomprehensible wedding (as incomprehensible as that of my own parents, which was also by proxy, the only photos showing my mother marrying Uncle Bernardo) Gilma Eusse smiled with the most cheerful, friendly face a person could imagine. She seemed the happiest woman in the world until one day she put a gun in her mouth and shot herself—no one knew why. But on those mornings of my childhood she'd help me roll the paper into the typewriter, so I could write. When my father came back from class I'd show him the result.

'Look what I wrote.'

There were a few lines of gobbledygook:

```
Jasiewiokkejjmdero
jikemehoqpicñq.zkc
ollq2"sa9lokjdoooo
```

'Very good!' my father would say with a satisfied chuckle, and congratulate me with a big kiss on the cheek, next to my ear. His kisses, large and resounding, deafened us and rang in our ears for a long time afterwards, like a memory at once happy and painful. One week he set me a task before he went off to teach: a page of vowels, first *A*, then *E*, and so on; and over the following weeks he introduced more and more consonants, the most common to start with—*C*, *P*, *T*—and then all the rest, even *X* and *H*, which although silent and rarely used, was very important because it was the first letter of the name we share. As a result, when I started school I already knew all the letters of the alphabet, not just by name but by sound. When the first grade teacher, Lyda Ruth Espinosa, taught us to read and write, I learned in a second, understanding the mechanism straight away, as if by magic, as if I'd been born to read.

There was one word, however, that I could not get into my head, and it took me years to learn to read it correctly.

Every time it appeared in print (thank goodness not often) my mind went blank, and my voice wouldn't work. I trembled in dread whenever I saw it coming, sure I wouldn't be able to pronounce it properly. It was the Spanish word for parish priest: *párroco*. I didn't know where the stress fell, and absurdly, almost always put it on rolling the R—'*parrrrrroco*'—rather than on one of the vowels. Or I might say '*parróco*,' with the stress in the middle, or '*parrocó*,' with the stress at the end. In any case, never '*párroco*.' My sister Clara took inordinate delight in teasing me about this mental block, and was forever writing the word down and asking me, with a radiant smile: 'Chubby, what does it say here?' As soon as I saw the word I'd turn red and not be able to read it.

It was the same, years later, when it came to dancing. My sisters were all great dancers, and like them I had a good ear, at least for singing, but when they asked me to dance I'd get the stress all wrong, keeping time only with their laughter at my total lack of rhythm. And although there came a day when I learned to read *párroco* correctly, dance steps have forever eluded me.

It is difficult enough to have just one mother; I can't tell you what it was like to have six. I think my father understood early on that making fun of me was certain to put me off anything for good, that if I even suspected that what I was doing might appear ludicrous or laughable, I would never try it again. When he celebrated even the meaningless gobbledygook I wrote, teaching me slowly and patiently how each letter represented a sound, perhaps it was so that my early errors wouldn't provoke laughter. On his typewriter I learned the whole alphabet, the numbers and all the punctuation marks, which may explain why a keyboard—much more than a pencil or pen—is for me the truest representation of the act of writing. That way of going along pressing sounds, as on a piano, to convert ideas into letters and words, seemed to me from the start—and still seems to me—one of the most extraordinary acts of magic in the world.

Besides, my sisters, blessed with the incredible linguistic ability of women, never let me speak. I only had to open my mouth to say something, and they'd already said it, in more detail and much more wittily and intelligently than I ever could have. Sometimes it seems to me that I learned how to write only so that I could communicate every once in a while.

From a very early age I wrote letters to my dad, which he celebrated as if they were Seneca's epistles or masterpieces of literature. Now, when I realize how limited my writing talent is (I almost never succeed in making my words as clear as the ideas in my thoughts, and what I do strikes me as poor and clumsy, mere stuttering compared with my sisters' articulacy), I remember the confidence my father had in me. Then I straighten my shoulders, and on I go. If he liked even my scribbles, what does it matter if what I write doesn't entirely satisfy me? I think the only reason I've been able to keep writing all these years, and to commit my writings to print, is because I know my father, more than anyone, would have enjoyed reading these pages of mine that he never got to read, and that he'll never read. It is one of the saddest paradoxes of my life: almost everything I've ever written has been for someone who cannot read me, and this book itself is nothing more than a letter to a shade.

4

There was one custom in my house that even the laughter and teasing of my friends and classmates could not eradicate. When I got home from school, my father would greet me with hugs, kisses and all sorts of endearments, winding up in a contented chuckling. The first time my friends witnessed it they laughed at this 'faggoty pampering.' This insult took me by surprise. Until that moment I had believed that all fathers greeted their sons this way. But no—it turned out that in Antioquia this was not the case. A greeting between father and son had to be distant, rough and without apparent affection.

For some time I was embarrassed and avoided these effusive greetings if there were strangers around, not wanting to be laughed at. But I missed my father's hugs and kisses, which made me feel safe, so after a while I let him greet me as he always had. My classmates could laugh and say whatever they liked: after all, this affectionate greeting was my father's thing, not mine—I merely allowed him to do it. And besides, not all my classmates ridiculed me: I remember one, when we were nearly grown up, confessing: 'Man, I've always wished I had a father like yours. Mine hasn't kissed me once in my whole life.'

'You write because you were a spoiled child,' someone who called himself a friend once said to me. He said it in English, to sharpen the gibe, and although it infuriated me, I think he was right.

My father always thought—and I agree and imitate him—that indulging one's children is the best system of education. In a book of notes that I assembled after his death under the title *Manual of Tolerance*, he wrote the following: 'If you want your son to be good, make him happy, if you want him to be better, make him happier. We make our children happy so they'll be good and so their goodness then increases their happiness.' It's possible that no one, not even parents, can make their children completely happy. What is certainly true is that they can make them very unhappy. He never hit us, not even lightly, and was very permissive—what people in Medellín call *un alcahueta*, a pushover. Indeed, I might almost say he showed me too much love, though I'm not sure if excess exists when it comes to love. Perhaps it does, since after all there are unhealthy loves, and something often repeated to raise a laugh at family gatherings is one of the first sentences I ever spoke, still in baby talk:

'Daddy, don't adore me so much!'

Years later, when I read Kafka's *Letter to his Father*, I remember thinking that I could write the same letter, only its exact opposite, just using antonyms and turning the situations the other way round. My father didn't frighten me, but inspired trust; he wasn't a despot but tolerant with me; he didn't make me feel weak, but strong; he didn't think me stupid, but brilliant. Without having read one story, much less a book of mine, he divined my secret and told everyone I was a writer, though it infuriated me that he treated as fact what was only a dream. How many people can say they had the father they would wish for if they were born again? I can.

I now believe the more love one receives from one's parents in childhood, the better one copes with the vicissitudes of life. Without the disproportionate love my father gave me, I would have been a much unhappier person.

Many people complain about their fathers. In my city there is a terrible saying: 'A man only has one mother, but his father could be any old son of a bitch.' I might, perhaps, come close to agreeing with the first half of this sentence, taken from a tango lyric, even though, as I've explained, I myself had half a dozen mothers. But with the second half, I utterly disagree. In fact, I think I even had too much of a father. My father was, and in a way continues to be, a constant presence in my life. I find myself obeying him even now—though not always, for he also taught me how to disobey if necessary. When I'm mulling over something I've done or am going to do, I try to imagine what my father would have said, and have resolved many moral dilemmas simply by appealing to the memory of his attitude to life, his example, and his words.

I don't mean to give the impression that he never told us off. His voice was like thunder when he got angry, and he thumped the table with his fist if we spilled something or said something stupid during dinner. In general he was very indulgent towards our weaknesses if he considered them incurable, like an illness. But if he thought it was something we could correct, all his in-dulgence vanished. His professional interest in hygiene meant he couldn't stand us being dirty, and he made us wash our hands and clean our nails in a ritual that seemed practically pre-surgical. Above all, he hated it if we displayed a lack of social conscience or understand-ing of the country we lived in. One day when he was ill and couldn't make it in to the university, he was upset that a lot of students would have paid the bus fare to class for nothing, so I said:

'Why don't you phone them and let them know?'

He went white with rage.

'What part of the world do you think you live in? Europe? Japan? Or perhaps you think everyone lives in neighbourhoods like Laureles? Don't you know there are parts of Medellín where they don't even have running water, let alone a telephone?'

I remember another of his rages, a lesson as hard as it was unforgettable. At the age of ten or twelve, a group of local kids somehow got mixed up in a loutish expedi-tion, a sort of miniature *Kristallnacht*. Diagonally oppo-site our house lived a Jewish family—the Maneviches. The bossiest kid on the block, a big boy with a shade of down on his upper lip, made a plan to go and stand out-side the Jews' house to throw stones and shout insults. I joined the gang. The stones weren't very big, bits of gravel really, and scarcely made a noise against the win-dow panes, much less broke them. As we threw them we shouted a phrase whose origins I've never known: 'Hebrews eat bread! Hebrews eat bread!' Perhaps it was meant to be some kind of cultural affirmation of the *arepa*, the cornmeal rolls we ate. One day my father came home from the office while we were doing this. Enraged, he jumped out of the car, grabbed me by the arm with a violence I had never before known, and dragged me to the front door of the house.

'You don't do that! Ever! We are going to speak to Señor Manevich right now, and you are going apologize to him.'

He rang the bell. A very pretty, haughty girl, older than me, answered, and eventually a sullen and aloof Señor César Manevich came to the door.

'My son is going to apologize to you, and I assure you this will never happen again,' my father said.

He squeezed my arm and, looking down at the floor, I said: 'Sorry, Señor Manevich.'

'Louder!' insisted my father, and I repeated louder: 'Sorry, Señor Manevich!' Señor Manevich nodded very slightly, shook hands with my father and closed the door. I had a scratch on my arm, the only mark my father ever left on my body. It is a mark I deserved and the memory of which still shames me, not only because of everything he was to tell me later about the Jewish people, but also because my brutal, idiotic act had been prompted solely by a herding instinct and not by any genuine opinions, good or bad, about Jews. Perhaps this shame is at the root of my adult rejection of groups, parties, associations and mass demonstrations—all gangs that might lead me to think and act not as an individual but based on this weakness, the desire to belong to a crowd.

When we got back from the Manevich family's house, my father—as he always did at important moments—took me into his study with him and shut the door. Looking me straight in the eye, he said the world was still full of a plague called anti-Semitism. He told me what the Nazis had done to the Jews scarcely twenty-five years earlier, and that it had all begun with the act of throwing stones at windows, during the terrible *Kristallnacht*, or night of broken glass. Then he showed me some terrifying pictures of the concentration camps. He said that his best friend and classmate, Klara Gottman, the first female doctor to graduate from the University of Antioquia, was Jewish, and that some of the greatest geniuses humanity had produced over the last century, in science, medicine and literature, had been Jewish. If it weren't for them there would be much more suffering and much less happiness in this world. He reminded me that Jesus himself was a Jew, and that many Antioquians—possibly including ourselves—had Jewish blood, because all the Jews in Spain had been forced to convert. It was my duty to respect and treat them like any other human being, or even better, because the Jewish people, along with the indigenous peoples of the Americas, black people and gypsies, were among those who had suffered the worst injustices over the last few centuries. And if my friends insisted on such barbaric behaviour, I could never play with them in the street again. As it turned out, this threat was unnecessary: the other children had observed 'how furious Dr. Abad was' from across the road, and that was enough to deter them from throwing stones or shouting insults at the Manevich family's windows ever again.

5

When I started kindergarten, with its strict rules, I felt abandoned and mistreated. It was as if I'd been sent to jail without having committed a crime. I hated going to school: the queues, the desks, the bell, the timetables, the Sisters' threats at the mere suggestion of happiness or hint of freedom. My first school, La Presentación—which my mother had attended and where all my sisters studied—was a convent school. Boys were admitted for the first two years of kindergarten, before the start of elementary school, even though it was a girls' school. We were, however, overwhelmingly in the minority, an endangered species. I don't remember a single boy among my classmates, so for me school was like an extension of home: women, women, and more women. The one exception was on the bus, where there was the driver and another little boy; dressed in our white shirts and dark blue shorts, we would sit together on one of the back seats. For the entire journey this little boy would take his willy out from one side of his shorts, and rub it and scratch it and pull at it non-stop, and he did the same on the way back, all the way from school until the bus dropped him off at his house. I didn't dare to say anything, but simply watched in amazement, unable to understand this behaviour. Indeed, I still don't understand it now, and have never forgotten it.

Every morning I waited for the school bus in the doorway, but when it nosed around the corner, my heart trembled and I ran inside, terrified.

'Where are you going?' Sister Josefa shouted furiously, trying to grab me by my shirt.

'I'm coming. I'm just going to say goodbye to my dad,' I replied from the bottom of the staircase.

I ran up to his room, into the bathroom (where he would be shaving), hugged his knees and started to kiss him, supposedly to say goodbye. But the farewell ceremony lasted so long that the bus driver would grow tired of honking his horn and waiting, and by the time I came downstairs, the bus would have gone, and I would no longer have to present myself at La Presentación. Another day of respite! Sister Josefa would get angry and say that if they kept spoiling me, I would never amount to anything, but my father always replied with a chuckle: 'Calm down, Sister, everything in its own time.'

This scene was repeated so often that eventually my father took me into his study, looked me in the eye and asked me, very seriously, if I didn't actually want to go to school yet. I said I didn't, and immediately school was delayed for a year. It was wonderful, such an immense relief that even now, forty years later, I feel light-hearted when I remember that moment. Was he wrong? I can assure you that the following year there wasn't a single day when I wanted to stay at home, and from that point on I never missed school unless I was ill. In all my years of elementary, secondary and university education I never failed a subject. 'The best form of education is happiness,' my father used to say, perhaps with an excess of optimism. But he said it because he truly believed it.

The following year, the bus never left without me. Or rather, I missed it just once, a day I'll never forget. A few weeks after starting back at the same convent school—the second attempt at weaning me—I remember a dreamy mood stole over me at breakfast one morning. I spent ages savouring the taste of my fried egg yolk, and the bus drove off without me. I saw it turn the corner, and though I ran after it, nobody on the bus heard my shouts. No one in the house realized the bus had gone without me and I didn't want to go back in, so I made up my mind to walk to school instead. La Presentación was in the city centre, on Ayacucho, close to San José church, where the police have their headquarters now. I walked down Carrera 78, where we lived, to 33rd Avenue, and set off in vaguely the right direction.

As I crossed over the Bulerías roundabout, cars honked their horns at me and a taxi had to brake hard, its tyres screeching as it barely avoided hitting me. I was sweating, with my leather satchel on my shoulder, walking as fast as I could along the side of the road. The roundabout had been an almost insurmountable obstacle, but I'd overcome it and carried on towards the river, where I thought the bus usually went. I stopped for a minute to rest on the bridge over the River Medellín, at the bottom of Nutibara Hill, and stared through the railings at the water flowing by. If my father ever died, I planned to throw myself into this very river. I'd never seen it up so close, so dirty, so ominous. Before getting my breath back, I started walking again, along the side of the road. At that moment—I can still hear it now—

there was a second screech of brakes at my side. Was I about to be killed by another taxi? No. A man in a Volkswagen, introducing himself as René Botero, called to me from his window: 'What are you doing here, kid? Where are you going?' 'To school,' I said. 'Get in and I'll drive you,' he yelled furiously, 'before you get killed by a car or snatched!' I was still several miles away from La Presentación, and we didn't exchange another word during the fifteen-minute journey.

That evening I got a long telling-off from my mother. She told me I was crazy to try to walk into town by myself, without even knowing the way. Across the river was Barrio Triste, where I would have got hopelessly lost. If it hadn't been for René Botero, a neighbour, I wouldn't be here now to tell the tale.

Later my father, instead of telling me off, said: 'If you ever miss the bus again, for whatever reason, even if it's your own fault, ask me to drive you, and I'll take you. Always. If I can't, you can just stay home and not go to school for a day. And that's fine too: you can read, and learn even more.'

Weaning myself from home was a lengthy process. At the age of twenty-eight, when my father was killed, I was still receiving the odd contribution from him or from my mother, though I had already been living with my first companion for five years, and had a daughter taking her first steps. When, aged twenty-three, I followed my Italian girlfriend, Bárbara, to Turin to study, I wrote a letter to my father expressing my worries about the fact that he still had to support me. I still have his reply, dated 30 June 1982 (I had left for Europe fifteen days earlier):

'Your concern about your prolonged *financial dependency* reminded me of my anthropology classes, where I learnt that the more advanced a species, the longer its period of childhood and adolescence. And I think that our *family species* is pretty advanced in every sense of the word. I was also a *dependent* until the age of twenty-six, but this never worried me, to be honest with you. You can be certain that as long as you continue to study and work as you do, for us your *dependence* will not be a burden but rather an agreeable duty that we undertake with a great deal of pleasure and pride.'

6

My father and I had a physical fondness for each other that many of those close to us thought scandalous and possibly unhealthy. Some of my relatives said my father's indulgence would make me 'queer.' And my mother, perhaps to compensate, tried to favour my five sisters, treating me with righteous severity and dedicating far more time and attention to them. Maybe my father's predilection for me was because I was the fifth child, and the only boy. Or perhaps it was really the other way round, and it was my predilection for him that sparked his preference. Parents do not love their children equally, though they pretend to, but generally love most the children who most love them—that is, deep down, who most need them. In favouring me, particularly by engaging me more than my sisters in serious conversation, my father (I admit he wasn't perfect) was revealing a deep-seated machismo and committing an act of injustice.

The block we lived on was colonized by the Abad family. Our family lived on the top corner of Calle 34A and

79th; Uncle Bernardo's house was right next door, then Uncle Antonio's, and on the next corner, at Carrera 78, were our paternal grandparents, Antonio and Eva, who lived with their widowed daughter Aunt Inés, and another unmarried daughter, Aunt Merce, plus other more distant relatives who periodically came to stay: cousin Martín Alonso, a marijuana-smoking, hippy artist from Pereira, who later wrote a couple of readable novels; Uncle Darío, after his wife left him; two cousins called Lyda and Raúl, before they got married; our cousins Bernardo, Olga Cecilia and Alonso, who were orphans, and others like them.

I don't recall my uncles or my grandfather ever kissing their sons—if they did, it was only very occasionally. It was simply not done in Antioquia, with its austere mountain landscape devoid of all softness. My grandfather had raised my father with a whip and a firm hand, with no outward signs of affection, and this was how my uncles treated my male cousins (they were a little less rough with their daughters). My father never forgot the time grandfather had given him ten lashes with the leather reins of the horse that had just thrown him—'Let's see if you can learn to ride like a man'—or the times he sent him out to the fields in the middle of the night to bring in the livestock, for no other reason than to make him get over his fear of the dark and 'toughen him up.' There were no cuddles or caresses between them, not a shred of sympathetic understanding. If my male relatives ever displayed any paternal affection, it was on the last day of the year, after the New Year's pig had been roasted and eaten, and many shots of *aguardiente* had softened their hearts. By and large they addressed each other formally, with a ceremonial distance: expressions of affection between men were considered sentimental or effeminate, and only back-slapping or punches were allowed.

Grandma Eva used to say it was 'totally impossible to raise a child without the whip and the Devil,' and my mother, who used neither, often heard this piece of wisdom. My grandfather, too, would say from time to time that what I needed was a 'firm hand,' to which my father would reply: 'If that is what he needs, he'll get it from life, which ends up being hard on us all. Life provides more than enough suffering on its own, and I'm not going to add to it.'

When I think about it, I don't believe Grandpa Antonio was any less spoiled than I was, whatever he might say. Sometimes I would call at his house on Sundays, or on Monday nights, to collect the 'consignment.' This was a parcel of produce he brought each of his children from the hacienda in Suroeste: cassavas, lemons, eggs, little cheeses wrapped in *bijao* leaves, and above all grapefruits, mountains of grapefruits that my grandfather called *pamplemusas* and to which he attributed not only magical but—I later found out—aphrodisiac powers. When I showed up for the consignment, I would often find Grandma Eva on her knees before him, taking off his shoes. She did this every night, when he returned from the cattle fair (where he worked as a broker) or from his cattle-rancher's office—kneeling in front of him to remove his shoes and put on his slippers in a routine ritual of submission. Another of her duties was to get out his clothes in the morning, and lay them on the bed in the order he got dressed in: underpants, socks, shirt, trousers, belt, tie, jacket and white handkerchief. If she ever forgot to put them out—or set them down in the wrong order—Grandpa would fly into a rage and stand there stark naked, shouting what was he going to wear that day, damn it, and what good was a wife who didn't even know how to put her husband's clothes out!

His children and grandchildren felt a mixture of respect and fear for Grandpa Antonio. He was the richest, the tallest (at six foot one), and the whitest person in the family: with his fair hair and blue eyes, he was nicknamed 'Blondie Abad.' The only person who was not afraid of him, and able to counter his categorical statements, was my father, perhaps because he was the eldest son and had excelled academically and professionally. They were distant with each other, as if something had been broken in their shared past. I believe the way my father treated us was a silent, implicit protest at the treatment he had received from grandfather, a deliberate refusal to bring up his children the same way.

When I went to collect the consignment and was on my way out with the package of cassavas, little cheeses and *pamplemusas*, my grandfather would sometimes call to me: 'M'hijito, come here!' He would take out a leather purse he carried in his pocket and start huffing through his half-closed mouth, looking meticulously for the smallest coins, then hand me two or three, still huffing: 'Buy yourself a little something, *m'hijito*—or better still, save it for a rainy day.' My grandfather had saved all his life and had accumulated a small fortune, both from his cattle ranch south-west of Medellín, and from the livestock he shipped to the coast to graze on the pastures of other landowners, with whom he split the profits. When he acquired his thousandth calf, he threw a big party, serving bean stew, *aguardiente* and pork crackling to all comers. After his death, we never found out where these thousand calves were; my farmer uncles, who worked with him at the cattle fair, said there weren't really that many.

Three or four times a year I went with my grandfather to La Inés, the ranch he had inherited from his parents, in Suroeste, between Puente Iglesias and La Pintada. We drove there at dawn in a red Ford pickup truck, with Uncle Antonio at the wheel, me in the middle, and Grandpa by the window. He carried an otter-skin shoulder bag, made in Jericó, the village where he and my father were both born, and at some point during the journey he always showed me the six-shooter revolver he kept there, 'just in case.' There was also a secret pocket where he hid a wad of cash to pay the foreman and the ranch hands.

With its deadly weapon and its cash, the shoulder bag encapsulates other differences between Grandpa and my father. Don Antonio was always armed, whereas my father loathed guns and wouldn't even touch them. If he thought he heard the sound of burglars at night, my father would grab a pair of nail scissors from the bathroom and come out shouting, 'What do you want? What's going on?' And money always burned a hole in his pocket, so he never had big wads of notes. From him I inherited, or learned, the same aversion to guns, and the same difficulty in saving money, though this latter flaw is less generous in me, since I prefer to spend it than to give it away. In my grandfather's house there were said to be two forms of intelligence, 'the good kind' and 'the other kind,' which, although the word 'bad' was not used, was implicitly judged as such, since 'the good kind' (which some of my uncles and cousins had) served the worthy purpose of making money, while it—'the other kind'—only caused trouble and complicated one's life.

The final stage of the trip to the house at La Inés was a half-hour ride on horseback, and we were always met by the ranch hands with a drove of mules, a draught ox, and a collection of saddled-up horses. They waited for us next to a big, rambling house they called 'the garages,' because that's where our cars were left. They knew they had to be there every Thursday from ten in the morning, unless they received a message on Radio Santa Bárbara: 'The foreman of La Inés hacienda in Palermo is not to go out to the road this Thursday, because Don Antonio is not coming.'

In the car I would ask Grandpa Antonio which horse I was going to ride, and he always said the same thing: 'Stuck-stuck, my boy, you'll ride Stuck-stuck.' I found it strange that Stuck-stuck was a different colour and had a different pace each time I rode him, until I finally understood what my grandfather was saying when my cousin Bernardo, who was a bit older and much less naïve than I was, explained: 'You idiot! There's no such horse as Stuck-stuck. Grandpa just meant that children don't get to choose, they have to ride whatever horse they get stuck with.'

We would stay at La Inés until Saturday evening, and during the days I was happy, milking cows, riding horses and counting animals with the tip of my whip. I watched the farmhands as they went about their business: castrating the calves and foals, dipping the steers in special baths to get rid of their ticks, spreading methylene blue on the cows' swollen udders, or branding the bullocks with red-hot irons. Sometimes I'd take a dip myself, minus the insecticide, in the mountain stream, by a little waterfall two metres high they called 'Papa Félix's shower.' Papa Félix was my grandfather's grandfather, and they'd named the waterfall after him because, according to legend, he came down from Jericó twice a year, at Easter and at Christmas, to take his biannual bath.

I loved all these daytime activities, but at dusk, as the light gradually faded, I was filled with a nameless sadness, a sort of nostalgia for the whole world apart from La Inés. I would lie down in a hammock to watch the sun set, listen to the heartrending buzz of the cicadas and cry silently as I thought of my father with a melancholy that flooded my whole body. Meanwhile Grandpa would switch on the radio to listen to the Esso Reporter or the Gillette Sports Parade, whose devastating drone seemed to draw in the darkness, while he sat in a chair on the porch, panting in the heat and rocking endlessly to the rhythm of my despair.

When night had fallen my grandfather ordered the generator, a Pelton wheel turned by the current of the stream, to be switched on. This monotonous and constant drumming rhythm, and the wan, flickering light of the bulbs, was for me another image of sadness and abandon. Where I come from, this terrible affliction, where children suffer unbearably from their parents' absence, is called *mamitis*, but I secretly gave it another, more accurate name: *papitis*. The only person I missed, the person I cried for in those long, sad dusks at La Inés, was my papá.

When we returned to Medellín on the Saturday evening, my father would be waiting for me at Grandfather Antonio's house. He would greet me, laughing and shouting, with deafening kisses and suffocating hugs. Then he crouched down in front of me, gripped my shoulders, looked into my eyes, and asked me the question that most irritated my grandfather:

'Well, my darling, tell me: how did Grandpa behave himself?'

He never asked my grandfather how I had behaved; I was the judge of these trips. My answer was almost always the same ('Very well!') and this softened Grandpa's indignation. But one time I, a boy of seven, wiggled my open hand from side to side, as if to say 'so-so.'

'So-so? Why?' asked my father, opening his eyes wide, half worried, half amused.

'Because he made me eat corn porridge.'

'Ungrateful child!' Grandpa would say, huffing and puffing with indignation. This charge of ingratitude is one I've been forced to accept: all my life it has been one of my worst defects. But my father merely laughed with pleasure and took me to El Múltiple, where he bought me a vanilla and raisin ice cream 'to get rid of the taste of the porridge.' Later he told my sisters about Grandpa being 'so-so,' mimicking my side-to-side hand gesture and roaring with laughter at Don Antonio's indignant expression. Nobody ever forced me to eat anything at home, and today I eat everything. Except for corn porridge.

7

It was important to my father that his children knew that not everyone was as happy and fortunate as we were, and suffering was something I first experienced not personally or at home, but in other people. He thought it necessary for us to see from an early age that many Colombians suffered, mainly from the misfortunes and diseases associated with poverty. He spent some of his weekends working in the poor neighbourhoods of Medellín, and I remember when I was very young an American turned up at our house one day, a tall, charming, white-haired old man, Dr. Richard Saunders, who had decided, with my father, to set up a programme he'd already launched in other Latin American countries and in Africa. It was called *Future for the Children*. This kind gringo came to stay with us every six months, and when he entered the house I used to play the national anthem of the United States to welcome him. At home we had a record with orchestral performances of all the most important anthems of the world, from *The Star-Spangled Banner* and the *Internationale* to the National Anthem of Colombia, the ugliest of them all, although at school we were told it was the second prettiest in the world, after the Marseillaise.

The guest-room in our house was called 'Dr. Saunders's room,' and the best sheets in the house—I can still see them, pastel blue—were 'Dr. Saunders's sheets,' because they were only used when he came to visit. When Dr. Saunders was staying, the good porcelain china came out, the linen napkins and tablecloths embroidered by my grandmother, and the silver cutlery: 'Dr Saunders's china,' 'Dr Saunders's tablecloth' and 'Dr Saunders's silver.'

Dr. Saunders and my father spoke in English and I would listen, spellbound by the incomprehensible words and sounds. The first expression I learned in English was 'it stinks,' which I clearly heard Dr. Saunders say as we were crossing the River Medellín on the San Juan bridge. He said it in an indignant, offended murmur, prompted by a bus that was belching out a filthy, dense cloud of black smoke at the exact level of our noses.

'What does *it stinks* means?' I asked in Spanish. They laughed and Dr. Saunders apologized because it was a rude word.

'Something like *hediondo*,' my father replied.

And so I learned two words at the same time, one English and one Spanish.

My father used to take us to the poorest neighbourhoods of Medellín with Dr. Saunders (and many times without him, when he went home to Albuquerque). When we arrived, all the community leaders would gather, and my father would make various suggestions for action that could improve living conditions. These assemblies took place on a street corner, or in the presbytery if the parish priest invited them (though not all the clergy approved of this kind of social work). My father and Dr. Saunders would ask the community leaders questions about their problems and basic needs, with my father taking down their replies in a notebook. The first priority was always to organize clean drinking water for the neighbourhood, since children were dying of diarrhoea and malnutrition. I must have been five or six at the time, and my father would stand me next to children of the same age, sometimes older. He used me to show the community leaders that their children were thin, short and malnourished, and as a result would be unable to learn properly, not to humiliate them, but to stir them into action. He measured the circumference of newborn babies' heads, noted the results in tables, and took photos of skinny children with stomachs bloated from parasites, to use later in his classes at the university. He would also ask people to show him their dogs and pigs: if the animals were so famished you could see their ribs, it meant there wasn't a scrap of food to spare and people were going hungry. 'When there isn't enough food, we aren't even *born* equal,' he would say. 'These children are already at a disadvantage when they come into the world.'

Sometimes we went further, to outlying villages. On occasion we were accompanied by Dr. Antonio Mesa Jaramillo, Dean of Architecture at the Pontifical University, who would teach people how to make a proper water tank and connect pipes to their houses—drinking water always being the first priority. Next came latrines ('for the appropriate disposal of excrement,' my father would say, very technically), or if possible the construction of a whole sewer system, achieved at weekends through communal projects. Later there would be vaccination campaigns and 'home hygiene and first-aid' classes, part of a programme devised by my father with the help of the most intelligent and receptive women from each village and subsequently rolled out across the whole of Colombia under the name 'Rural Health Action.'

From time to time we'd be picked up by a university bus and all my father's students would come with us. He liked them to help and learn at the same time: 'We learn medicine not only by treating patients and studying cells in hospitals and laboratories, but also in streets and homes, where we can discover why people get sick and what from,' he would say very seriously from the first row of the bus, grasping a microphone.

Once, in the town of Santo Domingo, northwest of Medellín, they carried out a campaign against intestinal parasites that was so successful all the pipes in the village were blocked with the huge number of tapeworms the villagers expelled in one day. There is still a photo in my house of a sewage pipe blocked with a knot of tapeworms, like a clump of purplish-black spaghetti.

My father's obsession with clean water spanned his whole career, enduring until his death. In August 1945 he founded a student newspaper that ran for a little over a year, until October 1946, when it disappeared, perhaps because if he'd continued to publish it he wouldn't have been allowed to graduate. It was a tabloid that came out every month and had a futuristic name: U-235. In the May 1946 edition, he denounced the contamination of water and milk in the city. 'Medellín Council: A National Embarrassment' said the headline on the first page, with a subtitle adding: 'Aqueduct Spreads Typhoid Fever Bacteria. Undrinkable Milk. City Council Has No Hospital.' These denunciations were backed up by figures and evidence from the laboratory, and my father was invited to an open meeting of Medellín city council. It was the first time a lowly student had been admitted to take part in a public debate, to put his case to officials. Over two consecutive evenings, seated opposite the Health Secretary, he set out his points soberly and scientifically; the Secretary, unable to refute them, tried to duck the issue with personal insults and unimaginative arguments. But my father's intellectual victory was undeniable, and it had direct consequences. His calm words and precise facts were enough to get work started on constructing a decent aqueduct for the whole city (the one that still benefits us today), with proper water treatment and modern, sewage-proof pipes, to replace the old system, made of porous clay, which had been contaminating the drinking water.

His newspaper, and later his undergraduate thesis, also condemned the quality of the milk and soft drinks in the city. Hepatitis and typhus were still common in Medellín at the time of my father's revelations. Two of my mother's uncles had died from typhus caught from bad water, my grandmother had been ill from the same cause, and Grandpa Antonio's father had died of typhus in Jericó. Perhaps this explained my father's obsession with hygiene and drinking water; it was a matter of life or death, a way of preventing at least one sorrow in this world so full of fatal sorrows. But it was the death, again from typhoid fever, of one of his classmates at university that really sparked his fight for clean water. My father watched him slowly die, a boy who shared his hopes, and decided that this should never again happen in Medellín. His passionate denunciations in the student paper, and his strong words in the Council, deemed incendiary by some, were not 'political,' as was also claimed, but stemmed from his profound compassion for human suffering, and indignation at wrongs that could be avoided with just a little social action. This is what my father told the medical historian Tiberio Álvarez: 'I started to think about social medicine when I saw several children die in hospital, of diphtheria, and when I realized there were no vaccination campaigns ... Also when one of our classmates, Enrique Lopera, died of typhoid because chlorine had not been put in the aqueduct. Many people in a neighbourhood called Buenos Aires, where the girls are so pretty, were also dying of typhoid fever and I knew that this could be prevented by putting chlorine in the aqueduct ... I took a stand in the student newspaper U-235 and when they held the Open Council Meeting I called the councillors criminals because they were allowing the people to die of typhoid, by not having built a proper aqueduct. It was fruitful, as a great campaign for clean water followed: it was called Campaign H_2O, and as a result the aqueduct was improved and completed.'

The editorials in U-235 burn with the fervour of a romantic young idealist. Each issue champions some new and important cause. As a village boy newly arrived in the capital he could not realistically have expected to bring about huge change, but not only did my father fight for ideals that went beyond egotism (even if perhaps his noble stand itself contained traces of a different, more profound type of egotism), he also opened up his paper to other writers with similar aims and approaches.

Perhaps the most significant article published in U-235 appeared in the first edition. It was written by the greatest—maybe the only—philosopher our region has produced, Fernando González. My father described how he had started to read the 'thinker from Elsewhere' at a very early age, hiding the books under his mattress because once when my grandmother had seen what he was reading she had confiscated them and thrown them away. He had gone to see the master in his hometown of Envigado and asked him to write an article for his newspaper about the medical profession. González agreed, and the recommendations he made to doctors on this occasion were inked indelibly on my father's memory. For the rest of his life he tried, I think successfully, to live up to González's description of the ideal doctor:

The professor of medicine must be out on the road, observing, handling, seeing, listening, touching, struggling to heal, with a string of apprentices who reverently look up to him. Yes, young doctors: it is not about being kind and sending large bills and selling vitamin pills ... It is about sending you out to heal, to invent and, in a word, to serve.

8

As my father saw it, a doctor had to investigate and understand the relationship between patients' economic situations and their health, to stop being a witch-doctor and become a social activist and scientist. In his undergraduate thesis he denounced conjuror doctors: 'For them, a doctor must remain the supreme pontiff, eminent and powerful, who doles out familiar words of advice and consolation like a divine gift, who practises charity for the needy with the vague air of a priest descended from heaven, who is able to say the right thing at the inevitable hour of death and conceal his impotence behind Greek terminology.' He was angered by those who wanted simply to 'apply treatments' to typhoid fever, rather than preventing it by improving hygiene, and he was exasperated by the 'marvellous cures' and 'new injections' which doctors bestowed on their high-paying 'private clientele.' He felt the same antipathy towards those who merely 'healed' children, instead of operating on the true social causes of their illnesses.

My older sisters recall, though I don't, being taken to San Vicente de Paúl Hospital. Maryluz, the eldest, clearly remembers one time my father took her to the Children's Hospital and made her walk through the wards, visiting one ill child after another. My sister says that he seemed almost like a madman, or a maniac, stopping in front of nearly every patient and asking: 'What's wrong with this child?' Then he would answer his own question: 'He's hungry.' And a bit further on: 'What's wrong with this child?' 'She's hungry.' 'What about this one?' 'The same thing: hunger.' 'And this one?' 'Nothing but hunger. The only thing wrong with all these children is that they're hungry, and an egg and a glass of milk a day would be enough to keep them from being here. But we're not even capable of giving them this: an egg and a glass of milk! Not even this! It's inhumane!'

His laboratory research revealed amoebas, TB bacteria and faecal matter in the milk sold in Medellín and the surrounding villages. By acting on his compassion, and his firm belief that hygiene could be improved through education and public works, he managed, while still a student and despite strong opposition by cattle farmers worried about losing money, to make it obligatory to pasteurize milk correctly before sale. He argued that the simple provision of drinkable water and clean milk would save more lives than individual curative medicine, though this was the only sort most of his colleagues wanted to practice, partly to get rich and partly to increase their magician-like prestige within the tribe. According to my father, operating rooms, surgery, the most sophisticated diagnostic techniques (to which only a few people had access), specialists of all kinds, and even antibiotics themselves— wonderful as they were—saved fewer lives than clean water. He put forward the basic idea—basic but revolutionary, being of benefit to the masses rather than to a small minority—that water is the most important thing, and that resources shouldn't be spent on other things until everyone had access to drinkable water. 'Epidemiology has saved more lives than all therapies put together,' he wrote in his thesis. Many doctors detested him for putting clean water before their grand projects for private clinics, laboratories, new diagnostic methods and specializations. It was a deep hatred, no doubt aggravated by the government's perpetual wavering about how to distribute its scant resources: if my father's aqueducts were built, they wouldn't be able to buy their sophisticated pieces of apparatus or build their hospitals.

It wasn't just a few doctors who hated my father; his work was generally frowned upon in the city. His colleagues would gripe that 'you don't need a medical degree to do what this "doctor" does'; for them medicine was treating ill people in their private practices. To the richest it seemed that, with his mania for equality and his social conscience, my father was organizing the poor to start a revolution. When he went out into the countryside and tried to persuade the agricultural labourers to carry out communal action, his critics in the city claimed he spoke too much about their rights, and too little about their duties. When had the poor ever been known to protest? A very important politician, Gonzalo Restrepo Jaramillo, said in the Union Club—Medellín's most exclusive—that Abad Gómez was the best-organized Marxist in the city, a dangerous left-winger who should have his wings clipped. My father had attended a down-to-earth, pragmatic North American college (the University of Minnesota), had never read Marx, and often got Hegel mixed up with Engels; but now, to find out what he was being accused of, he resolved to read them all. When he did, not all their ideas seemed so preposterous to him, and over the course of his life, he very gradually, and only partially, turned into something akin to the left-wing fighter his accusers imagined him to be. Towards the end of his life he used to say he was an ideological hybrid: Christian in religion, because of the kindly figure of Jesus and his obvious compassion for the weakest people in society; Marxist in economics, because he detested financial exploitation and the disgraceful abuses of capitalists; and liberal in politics, because he couldn't abide lack of freedom or dictatorship, even that of the proletariat, since when the poor came to power, and stopped being poor, they were no less despotic and ruthless than the rich when they were in charge.

'That's right, a hybrid. Half cow and half horse—can't trot and produces no milk,' teased Alberto Echavarría, a haematologist at the university where my father worked, and father of Daniel and Elsa, my best friend and first girlfriend respectively.

At the university the authorities often criticized my father and schemed to make his life difficult. Depending on the Rector or Dean at the time, he either worked in peace or amid thousands of complaints, recriminating letters and veiled threats of dismissal. Although he attempted to deal with them all, or at least to laugh them off, there came a time when laughter wasn't enough.

My mother remembers with particular clarity one of these many attacks, from Dr. Jaramillo, a prestigious professor and head of cardiovascular surgery at the university. Once in a meeting, with my mother and father present, Jaramillo said with great emphasis: 'I won't breathe easy until I see Héctor hanging from a tree in the University of Antioquia.' A few weeks after my father had been killed, something many people had long wished for, my mother bumped into this professor in the supermarket. She walked up to him in the meat aisle and said, very slowly and looking him straight in the eye: 'So, Dr. Jaramillo, can you breathe easy now?' He went pale and, not knowing what to say, turned around and walked away with his trolley.

A few priests were also obsessed with my father, and were constantly attacking him. There was one in particular, Father Fernando Gómez Mejía, who hated him with all his heart. His hatred had all the faithfulness and constancy that one could ever wish for in love, and it had become an irrepressible passion. He had a regular column in the Conservative daily *El Colombiano*, and every Sunday presented the radio programme 'Catholic Hour.' This priest was a fanatical troublemaker, a disciple of the reactionary bishop from Santa Rosa de Osos, Monsignor Builes. He suspected everyone of committing terrible sins of the flesh, and dealt out anathemas left and right, in an irritating drone so high-pitched and monotonous that his programme became known as 'Sour-Hour.' He dedicated at least fifteen minutes of this hour every month, as well as several columns over the years, to ranting about the danger of the 'communist doctor' who was infecting the minds of the people in the city's poor neighbourhoods. According to him, my father, merely by making people aware of their poverty and their rights, was 'injecting the poison of hatred, bitterness and envy into the simple minds of the poor.' My mother fretted about this, and although my father always tried to laugh it off, deep down it bothered him.

One time he didn't laugh. The priest read out a communiqué from the Archdiocese of Medellín, directed against my father and signed by the archbishop himself.

9

My mother was the daughter of the archbishop of Medellín, Joaquín García Benítez. Now I know that sentence might seem blasphemous, since Catholic priests practised celibacy—at least they did back then—and the archbishop was the most celibate and strict of them all. In fact, my mother was not his daughter; she was his niece. But, being an orphan, she had spent a large part of her childhood and adolescence with him, and always said that Uncle Joaquín had been like a father to her.

We lived in an ordinary house in Laureles, but she had grown up at 'the Palace' with Uncle Joaquín; this was the biggest and most ostentatious house in the city centre, originally named Amador Palace, for the rich merchant who had built it at the turn of the last century, importing the building materials from Italy and the furniture from Paris. When Amador's son died, the Curia purchased the mansion and renamed it 'The Archbishop's Palace.' Uncle Joaquín was large and slow-moving, like a gentle ox, spoke with guttural 'r's, like the French, and had such a prominent belly that a curved niche had to be cut into the head of the table so he could sit comfortably in the dining room.

There was a legendary tale from his past, from the 1920s, when he'd been working in Mexico. He had founded a new seminary in Xalapa, where he was the general prefect, as well as Professor of Sacred Theology, Latin and Spanish. At home we were told that during the Cristero War—fought between the Mexican government and thousands of recalcitrant Catholics stirred up by the Vatican's opposition to the 1917 Constitution— Uncle Joaquín had fled the seminary (where some of the nuns had been treated dishonourably by government soldiers) and hidden in Papantla. He was captured there and condemned to death, but as he faced the firing squad they commuted his sentence, because he was a foreigner, to twenty years in prison. No one knows how he managed to escape, but he was caught again in Papantla, by General Gabriel Gaviria, a follower of Pancho Villa, and sent to another prison. He escaped again, with the help of some devout women, and it was said he arrived in Havana, where his brother was the consul, in a rowing-boat that he and some other persecuted priests took from Veracruz. The story goes that they had rowed across the Gulf of Mexico, prevailing over the wild waves of the Caribbean with nothing but the strength of their own arms.

My mother always spoke of the Palace and her Uncle with reverence: you could hear the capital letters in her voice. When she and Emma, the cook, were making something special in the kitchen—say a really complicated sapote ice cream, some never-ending Santander tamales, a laborious asparagus salad with *curuba* juice, or an elaborate mandarin liqueur that had to be buried in an earthenware jar for four months—my mother would say: 'This is a Palace recipe.' My father used to tease her: 'Why is it that when we were courting and you lived in the Archbishop's Palace the most sophisticated thing I got to eat was stewed mulberries with a glass of milk?' and then he laughed in his usual way.

Towards the end of his life, the archbishop gradually lost his memory. Sometimes, in the cathedral, he would lose his train of thought and skip parts of the Mass; or, worse still, his mind would go blank after the Elevation and, without realizing, he'd go back and start over again: *In nomine Patris et Filii* ... Back then, years before the Second Vatican Council, priests said Mass with their backs to the faithful and in Latin. Some of the members of the congregation felt sorry for their cleric, while others laughed at him. Some of the priests who assisted in the archdiocese took advantage of his memory lapses, and on one occasion a secretary, who detested my father, gave him a letter to sign. Uncle Joaquín signed the piece of paper without reading it, because he trusted his subordinate and thought it was a routine document. It turned out to be a communiqué attacking my father for his 'socialist' activities in the poor neighbourhoods of Medellín, and for his 'incendiary' articles in the newspapers, 'full of irreligious maxims opposed to wholesome practices and apt to destroy the morals in minds still lacking in judgement, and of lethal and impious toxins that seek to incite rebellious uprisings and national disorder.'

My mother heard the communiqué on 'Catholic Hour.' Trembling with rage and fear, she immediately picked up the telephone and called her uncle to ask why he had signed this harsh and unjust attack on her husband. Uncle Joaquín didn't have the faintest idea what he had put his name to. Although he disagreed with everything my father said or wrote, for he was an old-fashioned, uncompromising bishop (he banned films that showed an ankle, and vetoed, on pain of excommunication, the visits of actresses and female singers to the city), he didn't have it in him to admonish publicly someone who, to all intents and purposes, was his son-in-law.

When he saw his signature stamped on this communiqué (with which he agreed, although he would never have wanted to publicize his views in that way), Uncle Joaquín felt betrayed, and became so indignant that after a few days he resolved to compose a letter of resignation to the archdiocese. A few months later the letter of acceptance arrived from Rome. With a profound sense of failure and despair, and without a penny to his name (he had been one of the few bishops who took not only his vow of chastity but also his vow of poverty seriously), the archbishop retired to my grandmother's house. Eventually a group of well-to-do people in Medellín bought him a house of his own in Calle Bolivia, where he went to live with his brother and secretary, Uncle Luis. There, little by little, he slowly forgot everything, even his own name. His mind went blank, he stopped speaking, and shortly afterwards he died, exactly a month before I was born, having been perfectly silent for several months.

The day he died, my grandmother gave my father the archbishop's gold pocket watch, made in Switzerland but branded 'Antioquia Railway.' Today it belongs to me, since my mother gave it to me the day they killed my father, and it will pass, as a testimony and standard (though of what exactly I don't know), to my son, on the day that I die.

10

It was thanks to the archbishop, or rather, to his memory, that we had a nun to look after us at home, a luxury only the richest families in Medellín could normally afford. Uncle Joaquín had supported the foundation of a new religious order, the Sisters of the Annunciation, dedicated to caring for children, and as a thank you for his initial backing, Mother Berenice, the convent's founder and Mother Superior, sent Sister Josefa to our house, to help my mother take care of the younger children while she was setting up her office.

My mother and Mother Berenice were good friends. It was said that the Mother Superior could perform miracles, and when we went to the convent she would 'lay hands' on my mother, who suffered from migraines. She would let them rest on her head for a while, as she murmured unintelligible incantations. My younger sister and I would cower in the corner of her office, watching this ceremony in amazement and terror, expecting sparks to fly from her fingers at any minute. For a few days after each visit, my mother was cured, or at least claimed to be, and when many years later Mother Berenice died a saintly death, she was summoned during the beatification process to testify to these miraculous healings.

While Mother Berenice was still alive, Sol and I sometimes spent the weekend at the Sisters of the Annunciation convent. I remember the endless corridors, waxed and shining; the grounds and garden, with their fig trees and rose beds; the eternal and hypnotic prayers in the chapel, and the sharp scent of incense and candle wax that stung your nose. At the age of three or four, with her blonde curls and greenish-blue eyes, my little sister looked like a Renaissance angel, and once they dressed her up as a nun and got her to sing a song in the chapel called 'All alone I was one day,' which described the moment of the celestial call to a religious vocation. Forty years later, she can still recite it from memory:

All alone I was one day
In holy contemplation
When a voice to me did say
Religion's your vocation

Despite this early proselytizing, my sister Sol did not become a nun—although there is something fervent about her pious superstitions and sudden passions— instead qualifying as a doctor and epidemiologist. Listening to her I sometimes feel as though I'm hearing my father speak again: she goes on in the same way about clean drinking water, vaccinations, disease prevention and basic nutrition; it is as if history never moves forward but only in eternal cycles, and this were a country of deaf people where children still die of diarrhoea and malnutrition.

The convents of Medellín provided one of my father's acquaintances, a gynaecologist from the Faculty of Medicine, with a lucrative practice. According to a peculiar theory of his own invention, wombs not used for gestation grew tumours ('Women who don't bear children bear myomas'), and he determinedly set about removing the womb of every nun in the city, whether they had myomas or not. My father, with a mischievous impiety neither my mother nor Mother Berenice, let alone the archbishop, approved of, would joke that the doctor's motive was not to make money, but to avoid any awkwardness between the angels of the Annunciation and the 'Holy Spirit.' Then he'd laugh blasphemously and recite some famous lines by Antonio José 'Ñito' Restrepo:

A nun swelled up
After drinking holy water
And the swelling she had
Was a little holy daughter.

Before this, without anyone knowing how or when, nuns, even from the cloistered Order of Saint Clare, had from time to time become pregnant, and not by the Holy Spirit. But without a single monastic womb available in the whole province, this problem never reared its head again, and the chastity—at least apparent—of the nuns was guaranteed. Who knows, it may even be that this contraceptive method, far more drastic than all those prohibited by the Church, is still practised in a convent somewhere.

11

My mother came to realize that on a professor's salary, diminished by my father's boundless generosity, and under frequent threat of his sudden dismissal by the university board, it was impossible to maintain the family, at least to the levels of good taste and good food to which she'd become accustomed at the Palace. She decided to start work herself, supported by Mother Berenice's offer of free extra help in the house to set her mind at rest while she was out. This came in the form of our nanny-nun, Sister Josefa, who looked after Sol and me, the two youngest, on weekdays until we started school. My father, whose upbringing had left inevitable traces of machismo, didn't want my mother to work, or to acquire the physical and mental independence earning one's own money brings, but she managed to impose her wishes with her firm and unwavering nature, mixed with an indestructible and fundamental cheerfulness that is intrinsic to her, and makes her immune to bitterness and long-lasting quarrels.

Sometimes my mother took me to her office too. She didn't have a car, so we would take the bus, or my father would drop us off on the corner of Junín and La Playa on his way to the university. My mother had set up her tiny office in a broom cupboard, in a new building, La Ceiba, at the end of Avenida La Playa. At the time it was the tallest building in the city, and it seemed gigantic to us. We'd go up to one of the top floors in a big Otis lift, like the ones you find in hospitals; it was operated by lift attendants, beautiful black women always dressed in immaculate white, like nurses carrying out a mechanical task. I liked them so much that I would spend hours in the lift while my mother was working, going up and down next to those women who smelled of a cheap perfume that even now, when I catch a rare whiff of it, triggers a sort of nostalgic infantile eroticism.

My mother's office was located in the cleaners' storage room. It had a strong smell of soap and of air fresheners—round, pink, shiny tablets that smelled of camphor and were placed in the urinals—and there were boxes full of floor wash, bleach, broom handles, mops, and packets of cheap toilet paper, all stacked up in a corner. Sitting at a metal desk, my mother did all the building's accounts by hand, with a well-sharpened yellow pencil, in an enormous accountancy book with a hard green cover. She was also responsible for taking the minutes of the building's board meetings, writing them up in an antiquated style taught to her by Uncle Luis, the archbishop's brother, who had been the permanent secretary at the Academy of History: 'The illustrious cattle farmer Don Floro Castaño addresses the meeting to declare that toilet tissue should be used economically, in order that the shared expenses of the buildings' co-proprietors do not increase unnecessarily. The administrator, Doña

Cecilia Faciolince de Abad, notes that while Don Floro is entirely in the right, it is inevitable, due to physiological reasons, that a certain amount be used. Notwithstanding the aforementioned, the administrator informs the co-proprietors that one of their tenants, Dr. John Quevedo, has moved into his office, and is misusing it as a place of residence, and in the early hours of the morning makes use of the ladies' toilets on the sixth floor, where he proceeds to wash himself and, since he lacks a towel, also proceeds to dry his body with large quantities of toilet tissue, which, once used, he leaves upon the floor, for which reason ...'

My mother was an expert at typing and shorthand (she took dictation at an incredible speed, making marvellous indecipherable scrawls, like Chinese ideograms), as she'd done a secretarial course at the Remington School for Young Ladies, and before she was married she'd been secretary to the manager of Avianca Airlines in Medellín, Dr. Bernardo Maya. What's more, she used to tell us how the manager of Avianca was madly in love with her, and she had decided to marry Dr. Maya if my father, who at the time was doing his Master's in the States, didn't keep his promise and come back to marry her. On the rare occasion when my mother and father had an argument and stopped speaking to each other for an evening, my sisters would tease her by asking:

'Mum, do you wish you'd married Bernardo Maya?'

And one of the things that most worried me, as a child, was this unanswerable, or badly phrased question, of whether or not I would have been born, and how, if my mother had married, not my father, but Bernardo Maya. I was reluctant to renounce life altogether, so instead I tried to imagine that in such a case I wouldn't look like my father, but like Dr. Maya. But this conclusion filled me with horror, since if that had happened, and I didn't look like my father, but like Bernardo Maya, then I would no longer be myself, but another very different person, and so I wouldn't be who I was, and this was the same as not being at all. Dr. Maya lived very near our house, just around the corner, and he didn't have any children, which only increased my metaphysical terror at the thought of never having come into being. I regarded him with fear and suspicion. Sometimes we'd see him at Mass, looking as serious as a judge, and he'd say hello to my mother with a nostalgic and discreet movement of his hand, that seemed to come from long ago and far away. And since my father didn't go to Mass, it seemed to me that church was where my mother and Dr. Maya committed a terrible sin, that of saying hello to each other, as if each wave of his spurned hand was a secret signal of what might have been and was not to be.

Some time later, my mother's first assistant turned up at the office, a woman with a most appropriate name, given the circumstances: Socorro, which means 'help.' With her came the first adding machine, a little crank-operated device that astonished me, being able with just a few turns of its arm to solve all the arithmetic problems that took me hours to work out for my homework. Gradually, over the years, more and more employees arrived at the office, almost always women, including my three eldest sisters, until my mother's business had a staff of seventy women and managed most of the office buildings in Medellín. My mother moved out of the cleaning room in La Ceiba to a real office on the second floor of the same building, which she eventually bought, and from its new head office her business went on growing and improving. Today it occupies a large two-storey house, where my mother, after eighty well-lived years, still goes every day, from eight in the morning until six at night, driving her automatic car with the same skill and authority with which she waves her walking stick, like a bishop's crosier, and with almost the same enthusiasm as half a century ago when she filled her notebooks with those rapid and mysterious ideograms.

Male employees were rare in my mother's office and I think I was the first to infringe the unwritten but very wise rule, which says that the world would work much better if it were governed only by women. In any case, despite my gender, my mother hired me during the school holidays to help drafting letters, reports and minutes in the fictitious 'Reports and Correspondence Department.' It was there—writing business letters, drafting circulars with advice and complaints, battling with thorny issues (dog excrement, exposed adulteries, musical drinking sessions, the revealing of erect members in lifts and at windows, mariachi singers at four in the morning, partying mafiosos trying to pick up women, muggers from patrician families and drug addicts from puritan ones), polishing letters of condolence and resignation—that I underwent my longest and most difficult training for becoming a writer. A few of my friends who also went on to write books (Esteban Carlos Mejía, Maryluz Vallejo, Diana Yepes, Carlos Framb) went through this apprenticeship in the 'Reports and Correspondence Department' of my mother's business. It was a business she, with her feminist spirit, wanted to christen 'Faciolince & Daughters,' but which my father insisted be called 'Abad Faciolince Limited,' so that neither he nor I would be left out, as the women of the house seemed to have planned.

12

A few years after the archbishop's death, around the time I used to accompany my father and Dr. Saunders on their social work visits to Medellín's poorest neighbourhoods, The Great Mission made its solemn and noisy entrance into the city. The Mission represented another form of social work, the pious kind; a sort of Catholic Reconquest of the Americas backed by the Spanish *caudillo*, Generalissimo of the imperial armies and apostle of Christianity, His Excellency Francisco Franco. It was headed by a Spanish Jesuit, Father Huelin, a dark, abrupt man, who cut an ascetic figure, like Ignatius Loyola, founder of the Jesuits; drawn and with dark circles under his eyes, he possessed a lively, sharp and fanatical intelligence. His opinions were harsh and definitive, like those of an envoy from the Inquisition, and he was received in Medellín with great collective enthusiasm: someone sent from the other world to put right the disorder in ours by means of Marian devotion.

Along with the evangelists of the Spanish Reconquest

came a small statue of Our Lady of Fátima. At the time people were trying to consolidate its prestige as the most important devotional symbol of Catholicism. In order to save the world from Atheistic Communism, the Holy Father had requested that in the former Spanish colonies, and indeed throughout the whole world, the Holy Rosary be said fervently and with more diligence than ever. These were the days of the Cuban Revolution and Latin America's legendary guerrillas, who hadn't yet become bands of criminals devoted to kidnapping and drug trafficking, and still retained a certain heroic aura, for they defended programmes of radical reform and demanded social changes that were easy to agree with.

It was in order to counteract these destructive currents that Our Lady of Fátima was enlisted, as a supernatural aid that would redirect the masses along the path of devotion, of truth, of Christian resignation or of the very timid 'Social Doctrine of the Church.' More than poverty, water or agrarian reform, the apparition of the Most Holy Virgin in Portugal became the obligatory topic of conversation at home and in dressmakers, hairdressers and cafés. People engaged in all kinds of discussions, speculations and long theological arguments about the secrets revealed by the Most Holy Virgin to the three young shepherds from Cova da Iría to whom she had appeared. The Third Secret, a terrible secret known only by the third and last surviving shepherd girl and the Supreme Pontiff, was the one that really fired people's imaginations. According to the most popular hypothesis, hinted at darkly by the priests in their sermons, she had predicted the eruption of a Third World War between the United States and Russia: that is, between Good and Evil, a war that would be fought not with guns and cannons, but with atomic bombs, and would be like the final battle between God and Satan. We all had to be prepared for the ultimate sacrifice—and in the meantime say the Holy Rosary every day, pray that good would prevail, and that Russia, enemy of God and ally of the Enemy, would not be victorious. Many events on the world stage at that time seemed to back up this interpretation of the Third Secret as the coming of a Third World War, for we were often on the brink of catastrophe during those Cold War decades, whether for the most trivial reasons of human and nationalist pride, or through a simple nuclear accident.

The aim of the Great Mission was to spread the cult of Our Lady of Fátima throughout Latin America, and remind the masses of the goodness of Christian resignation: in the end God would reward the blessed poor in the next life, so the pursuit of wellbeing in this life was not urgent. Along with the Virgin came a comprehensive and vigorous plan to defend the eternal truths of the Catholic faith and to revive the moral values of the one true religion. Spain now had little political clout among our nations, but with the help of the Church the Generalissimo wanted to regain lost influence in the region: a kind of reconquest through faith, supported by the white, patrician families in each area. The initial drive consisted of several weeks of ceremonies, sermons in churches, the adoration of the statue brought from the Old World and blessed by the Holy Father, and meetings and retreats with the senior Catholics in each city. And with young people, professionals, journalists, sportsmen, political leaders ... This missionary work would be repeated in all the countries of Latin America, in further commemoration of the first evangelization of the Americas carried out by the conquistadors.

The campaign reached its peak in promoting the practice of the Dawn Rosary. At four o'clock in the morning, before sunrise, a large group gathered in front of the portico of the parish church and walked the streets of the neighbourhood, singing hymns and intoning the prayer to the Most Holy Virgin. The Medellín neighbourhood chosen by Father Huelin for the Dawn Rosary was Laureles, where we lived, since this was an up-and-coming neighbourhood of young bourgeois, upwardly mobile professionals, who might go on to achieve greater influence and social standing. The devotees set off at four in the morning, chanting, carrying candles and banging drums to attract attention. Father Huelin walked at the front, with the statue, banners and crusading standards waving in the wind, as the procession behind him said the Holy Rosary aloud. One or two thousand people, mainly women and children, walked through the neighbourhood to arouse faith in the Most Holy Virgin, and at the same time wake up the faithless residents who had overslept and were still in bed. My mother, Sister Josefa, the maids and my older sisters went on these processions; my father and I stayed at home sleeping like angels.

Dr. Antonio Mesa Jaramillo, Dean of Architecture at the Pontifical University, who used to go with my father and Dr. Saunders on their visits to the poor neighbourhoods of the city, was the first victim of the Dawn Rosary. One of the foremost architects in Medellín, he had lived in Sweden and had come back inspired with a passion for contemporary design. Irritated by this noisy display of faith (his belief was more restrained, and he practised his religion in private), he wrote an opinion piece for *El Diario*, the Liberal evening paper, in which he protested about the infernal racket made by the processions.

'Tambourine Christianity' was the title of his article, which was a furious critique of peninsular Catholicism. 'Was Christ a vociferous man?' he wondered, continuing: 'Once we could sleep, fall into nothingness, into the mystical space of slumber. Then Hispano-Catholicism came along to oppress our nerves. This is what Falangism is: noise, nothing, uproar. They confuse the religion of Christ with a bullfight. Early morning excesses, shrieks from the Dark Ages ...' My father shared this view, and used to remark sarcastically that the Eternal Father was not deaf and didn't need to be shouted at so loudly. Or if He was in fact deaf, as it sometimes seemed, it was a deafness not of the ears but of the heart.

As punishment for writing this article, Monsignor Félix Henao Botero, Rector of the Pontifical University, dismissed Dr. Mesa Jaramillo *ipso facto* from his post as Dean of Architecture, expelling him from the faculty forever and ever, amen. The newspaper *El Colombiano* carried out a survey among the city's intellectuals: almost all supported the Rector and harshly condemned the Dean's article. Only my father, introduced by the paper as 'the well-known left-wing leader,' praised Dr. Mesa Jaramillo's courage, declaring that, even if he didn't completely agree with him, as the citizen of a liberal country he was prepared to defend everyone's right to free expression, if necessary with his life.

My father, in whose own life the Church played only a marginal role, saw this kind of backwards Spanish Catholicism as very damaging to the country, with its persecution of independent-minded priests and believers who sought a more modern, open Catholicism. Among his acquaintances there had always been good priests— though the Church saw them as bad—with compassion for the problems of their community, especially in the poor neighbourhoods where we went on weekends. Father Gabriel Díaz was often cited by father as an example of a kind soul, a truly saintly person. Yet the bishops wouldn't allow him to work in peace, continually transferring him from one place to another when his parishioners started to love and follow him too much. Anyone who encouraged the poor to participate in politics or to wake up to their situation was considered a dangerous activist, and to be putting the unshakeable order of the Church and society at risk.

By the time the neighbourhoods of Medellín became a hotbed of killings and a breeding ground for thugs and hit men, a few years later, the Church had lost contact with these places, just as the State had. Both institutions had thought it best to leave them alone, and, left to their fate, they became places where savage hordes of murderers sprang up like weeds.

13

It had been several decades since an illustrious German philosopher had announced the death of God, but the news hadn't yet reached the remote mountains of Antioquia. More than half a century later, though, God was dying here too. Or at least a few youngsters were rebelling against Him and using shock tactics to prove that the Omnipotent One didn't care in the slightest what happened in this vale of tears (such as the *Nadaist* poets, who collected consecrated hosts, and let off stink bombs at Catholic writers' conferences), since neither were the reprobate punished by His wrath, nor were the good favoured by His grace.

In my own family, a similar war was being fought, between two belief systems: between faith in a furious God in his death throes, and belief in a nascent, benevolent reason. On one side were the sceptics threatened with Hellfire, and on the other the believers who claimed to be the defenders of good, yet who thought and acted with an often malevolent fury. This submerged war of old versus new convictions, this struggle between humanism and divinity, had its roots far back in my mother's family as well as in my father's.

My maternal grandmother came from ancient Conservative stock of discreet Christian habits. Her father, José Joaquín García, who was born in the middle of the nineteenth century and died at the start of the twentieth, was a schoolteacher who penned articles under the pseudonym Arturo, and wrote the magnificent *Chronicles of Bucaramanga*, as well as being president of the Directorate of the Conservative Party, honorary Belgian consul and vice-consul of Spain. Two of my grandmother's brothers were priests, one a bishop and the other a monsignor. A third, Uncle Jesús, had been a government minister during the long Conservative hegemony of the late nineteenth and early twentieth centuries, and the youngest was Plenipotentiary Consul in Havana for several decades. They had all sworn loyalty to the glorious party of their elders, the party of tradition, family and property. In spite of these origins, or perhaps because of them (her brothers' moral rigidity and scandalized disapproval of any worldly innovation always having annoyed her) my grandmother had married Alberto Faciolince, an affable, liberal, open-minded civil engineer. She had only a very short period of happiness with him, since after four years of marriage, just as my mother was beginning to talk, an accident had taken him suddenly to the bosom of God (then not yet dead) while building a highway close to Duitama in the department of Boyacá.

Shortly afterwards, in keeping with the Semitic tradition obvious in our customs if not our religion, one of Alberto's brothers, Wenceslao Faciolince, took his brother's widow as his wife. This Wenceslao was a bad-tempered lawyer, a judge in Girardota, who said, first thing in the morning, every single day: 'This is the awakening of a man condemned to death.' My grandmother was never happy with her new husband: he was nothing like his adored brother either in bed or at table, the two most important places in a house, and my mother (who because of him can't bear lawyers and passed this prejudice on to me) eventually killed him accidentally on purpose, by giving him an injection unsuitable for those with a heart condition.

Twenty years later my mother, having been raised by the archbishop according to the rules of the strictest catechism, reenacted her mother's story when she married another cheerful Liberal, my father, in a bid for freedom. For many of her relatives, especially her Uncle Jesús, the government minister, this was not an advisable marriage: for a young woman from a Conservative family to marry a Liberal was like a union of Montagues and Capulets.

I believe I can discern within my grandmother Victoria and my mother a certain tormented awareness of the contradiction of their lives. Both women were profoundly liberal in temperament: tolerant, ahead of their time, and without a trace of prudishness. They were joyful and dynamic, and believed in enjoying life before the worms eat us; by nature sociable and flirtatious, they had to conceal their spirit within external patterns of Catholic devotion and a facade of primness. My grandmother—in blatant contradiction to her brothers, all priests and Conservative party politicians—was a suffragist, and even claimed that one of the happiest days of her life was when, midway through the century, a supposedly totalitarian soldier established the vote for women (it isn't only families who are contradictory in this place; the whole country is riddled with paradox).

77

But she was unable to free herself from her old-fashioned upbringing, and so tried to compensate for her liberal temperament with an excessive show of fervour and commitment to the Church, as if she could simultaneously preserve both appearances and her own soul through the monotonous rosaries she repeated, and the vestments she sewed for the young priests of the poor parishes.

Something very similar happened to my mother, who was a feminist, if not in theory then in daily practice, as she had demonstrated by starting a business of her own, against my father's wishes, paying two girls to do the housework and going to work in an office, far from the economic guardianship and watchful eye of her husband.

Just as careers in the military, journalism, politics, or even literature can run in families, my mother's family had a calling to the priesthood in its blood. But with her generation, the solid rock of her family's religious unanimity—seemingly unbreakable since the days of the Conquest—had started to split. Two of her first cousins, René García and Luis Alejandro Currea, educated in the strictest principles of traditional Catholicism and ordained according to the custom of their ancestors, joined the Liberation Theologists and became rebel priests on the far left of the Church. Another of her cousins, Joaquín García Ordóñez, went to the other extreme, becoming the most reactionary priest in the whole of Colombia, which is saying something. As a reward for his retrograde zeal and his furious opposition to any kind of change, he was made a bishop and given the most traditionally Conservative diocese of the country, Santa Rosa de Osos, as heir to Monsignor Builes (a bishop for whom 'killing Liberals was a pardonable sin').

One of the rebel priests worked in a factory, where he tried to awaken the sleeping consciousness of the proletariat, and the other organized land invasions in the poor neighbourhoods of Bogotá, openly disobeying the Church hierarchy. I remember one night we went with my mother and father to the prison to take some blankets to René and Luis Alejandro. They had been thrown into La Ladera jail and were freezing to death in a squalid cell, accused of rebellion along with other priests from the Golconda Group, a movement drawing on the theories of Camilo Torres, the guerrilla priest, and which took seriously the Second Vatican Council's recommendation that the poor should be given preferential treatment.

I began to understand that a quiet war was being waged within the Church as well as all around it, and that it wasn't only in my house and my head that several factions were battling it out: things in the outside world were not so different. There were rebel priests in the poor communities who opposed not only unfettered capitalism, but were also against clerical celibacy, supporting abortion and the use of condoms, and later on the ordination of women and gay marriage.

Things were no clearer on my father's side of the family. Like his maternal counterpart, my paternal grandfather Antonio had been born into a traditional, Conservative family. His father Don Abad, was supposedly one of only three white men of Jericó—the only ones with the right to use the title Don. Antonio had dared to become the first Liberal anyone in the family could recall for over a century, and in doing so had to confront his own father-in-law, Bernardo Gómez, who'd been an officer of the Conservative army in the Thousand Days War and later one of the most recalcitrant Conservative senators. As a colonel, Gómez had fought against General Tolosa, a Liberal who according to my father's grandmother, 'was so evil he even killed Conservatives in their mothers' wombs.'

To escape the conservative orbit of his family and the Church, my grandfather had become a Freemason, thereby affiliating himself to a mutual aid organization apart from the Church, but whose members practised the same type of cronyism. Following several land disputes with his cousins, and to get away from the tittle-tattle, criticism and gossip of his family, he had sworn to have a complete blood transfusion, and change his surname from Abad to Tangarife, which he thought sounded less Jewish and more Arabic (a comic threat he never carried out).

Years later, during the mid-century period known as La Violencia, my grandfather would be threatened by police affiliated with the Conservatives in the north of the Cauca Valley, who were killing Liberals like him. He had moved the whole family to the town of Sevilla during the economic crisis of the 1930s. The arduous journey on horseback, with my grandmother Doña Eva pregnant, and my grandfather mad with pain from a peptic ulcer, took several days, and was remembered by my father as a biblical exodus with a joyous arrival in the Cauca Valley, the Promised Land 'where the Devil did not exist.' After many sacrifices, and by the sweat of his brow, my grandfather eventually managed to become a notary, and amassed something of a fortune in coffee and cattle farms.

The exodus from Jericó had been during my father's third year of primary school, but by the time they arrived in Sevilla my grandfather had decided that because they had talked so much on the way, and because his son was so intelligent, he could go straight into the fifth year, which is what happened. It was in Sevilla that my father received most of his basic education, and completed primary and secondary school. During his *bachillerato* in the Liceo General Santander, he became good friends with the school's rector, Dr. José María Velasco Ibarra, a famous Ecuadorian exile who had been president of his country several times, and my father always claimed this man had been one of the most important influences on his politics and life. All of his oldest friends were from Sevilla, but they were murdered for being Liberals, one by one, during La Violencia.

When my father returned to Colombia after graduating from Medical School in Medellín and completing his Masters in the United States, his whole family still lived in Sevilla. He started work in the Ministry of Health as head of the Transmissible Diseases Department and, during the presidency of the Conservative Ospina Pérez, had the idea of making a year's rural service obligatory for newly graduated doctors, drafting the bill that made this reform a reality. Meanwhile, back in Sevilla, at the beginning of La Violencia, his best friends from school, classmates from the Liceo General Santander, began to be murdered.

It was due to these crimes, above all the tragic death of one of his brothers-in-law, Aunt Inés' husband, Olmedo Mora, who was killed while fleeing from Conservative Party hit men, that my father and grandfather decided they must leave Sevilla and take refuge in Medellín, where the crime wave was less severe. Don Antonio was forced to sell off cheaply everything he'd acquired through twenty years of work and, by that time in his fifties, return to Antioquia to start over again. My father, having resigned from his post at the Ministry of Health with a furious letter (written in his customary tone of romantic indignation) in which he said he would not be an accomplice to the Conservative regime's murders, managed to secure an appointment in Washington as medical consultant for the World Health Organization. This fortunate exile saved him from the reactionary fury that killed four hundred thousand Colombians, including five of his best friends from high school. From that time on my father would declare himself 'a survivor of La Violencia,' lucky enough to be in another country during the harshest years of political persecution and the murderous conflict between the Liberal and Conservative parties.

The political turmoil and ideological tension would continue into my father's generation (and later that of his children). While my father had become a far more radical liberal than his father, one combining socialist and libertarian tendencies, another of Antonio's children, my uncle Javier, ended up being ordained as a priest in Rome and joining Opus Dei, the most far-right religious order of the time—and one that, contrary to the teaching of the Second Vatican Council, seemed to have opted to give preferential treatment to the rich.

This struggle between reactionary Catholicism and the principles of the Jacobin Enlightenment (combined with a belief in science-led progress) was also fought in my own home. During May, the month of the Virgin, my sisters, the maids, the nun and I, perhaps influenced by the Great Mission, would hold processions through the house. We placed a little statue of Our Lady of Perpetual Help, brought back from Europe for my mother by Uncle Joaquín, on a little silver tray with a crocheted doily and with a ring of flowers from the patio, while the nun sang:

On the 13th of May the Virgin Mary
Came down from heaven to Cova da Iría.
Ave, Ave, Ave Maria
Ave, Ave, Ave Maria.

With the Most Holy Virgin on our shoulders and candles in our hands, we proceeded through the hallways and all the rooms in the house. Wherever the Virgin entered, Satan would never penetrate, and so every week we began our procession from the back of the house, behind the laundry room and the washing line, where Emma's and Teresa's and Tatá's rooms were. Then we moved on to the ironing room, the kitchen, the pantry, the sewing room, the living room, the dining room, and finally, one by one, to the bedrooms on the second floor. The last room we visited, back downstairs, after we'd done the garage and the library, was 'Dr. Saunders's room.' He was Protestant, but no one held it against him, although Sister Josefa dreamt of converting him to the one true faith: the Catholic, Apostolic, Roman religion.

I took part in these processions, but in the evenings my father would counteract my daytime training with the encyclopaedia, and by talking and reading to me. As though I were a character in a play that dramatized the quiet struggle for control of my soul, I'd pass from the gloomy theological caverns of the mornings to the Enlightenment floodlights of the evenings. At the age when our most firm beliefs are formed, those that will probably go with us to the grave, I was lashed by contradictory gales. But all the while my true hero, secret and victorious, was the solitary nocturnal knight who with a teacher's patience and a father's love explained everything to me, under cover of darkness, with all the light of his intelligence.

The ghostly, obscurantist world that my days fed, full of otherworldly presences interceding for us before God, and with its idyllic or terrible or neutral afterlife, became by night, to my relief, a material world, more or less comprehensible by reason and science. Threatening, yes, since it couldn't help but be so, but threatening only because of natural catastrophes or the evil nature of some men. Not because of the intangible spirits that inhabited the metaphysical universe of religion, not because of devils, angels, saints, extraterrestrial souls and spirits, but because of palpable bodies and material phenomena. For me it was a relief to stop believing in spirits, lost souls and phantoms, not to be afraid of the Devil or fear God, and instead to focus my worries on protecting myself from thieves and germs, which one could at least confront with a stick or an injection, rather than the wispy defence of prayer.

'Go to Mass, so your mother doesn't worry, but it's all lies,' my father would say. 'If God really existed, he wouldn't care if people worshipped him or not—he isn't a conceited monarch who needs his subjects to kneel down in front of him. What's more, if he really were good and all-powerful, he wouldn't let so many horrible things happen in the world. We can't be completely sure whether God exists or not, and if he does we can't even be sure that He is good, or at least good to the Earth and to men. Perhaps we are important to Him in the way that parasites are to doctors or toads are to your mother.'

I was well aware that my father's life was dedicated partly to fighting and exterminating parasites, and that my mother had a secret and hysterical phobia of toads that meant we were forbidden from even pronouncing the name of this amphibian.

While Sister Josefa read me the sad story of Genevieve

of Brabant, which made me cry like a baby, and pious tales of other terrible martyrdoms from the whole catalogue of saints, my father read me poems by Antonio Machado, César Vallejo and Pablo Neruda about the Spanish Civil War. He told me about the crimes committed by the Holy Inquisition against poor witches (who couldn't really have been witches, because there were no such things as witches, or magic spells), about the burning of the unlucky monk Giordano Bruno (merely because he had claimed that Evil couldn't exist since everything was God and thus impregnated with God's goodness), and about the Church's persecution of Galileo and Darwin, for having removed Earth from the centre of the Universe and Man from the centre of Creation— Man who was no longer made in God's image and likeness, but in the image and likeness of animals.

At night I would repeat to my father what the nun had read to me in the afternoon, stories of the torture and sufferings of the saints, of terrible bonfires and violations of the flesh and severed breasts, and he would smile and say that, while it was true that the early Christian martyrs had suffered heroically, letting themselves be killed by the Romans to defend the cross and the idea of one true God, and although it was, perhaps, admirable that they had borne so steadfastly martyrdom by fire, lions or swords, their heroism was no greater or more painful than that of the indigenous people of Latin America, who had themselves been martyred by representatives of the Christian faith. The brutality and violence of Christians in Latin America was no less than that of the Romans against them in Old Europe: they had massacred indigenous people or fought against heretics and pagans with comparable savagery. In the name of the very same cross for which others had endured martyrdom, the Christian conquistadors had martyred other human beings and laid waste to temples, pyramids, and religions. They too had killed venerated gods, and made languages and entire peoples disappear, set on eradicating the evil that was represented by communities with different, mainly polytheistic faiths. And all this to impose, through hate, the supposed religion of love for one's neighbour, of a merciful God and brotherhood among men. In this *danse macabre*, where the victims of the morning became the executioners of the evening, the rival horror stories cancelled each other out, and I trusted only, with the optimism my father passed on to me, that the period we lived in would be less barbaric, a new era—almost two centuries after the French Revolution—of true liberty, equality and fraternity, when all human or religious beliefs would be peacefully tolerated, without the need to kill one another for these differences.

Although he taught me the shameful history of this warlike Christianity as a counterweight to the stories of its tortured martyrs, my father had a deep respect for the figure of Jesus himself, in whose teachings he found nothing morally contemptible, except that they were almost impossible to obey, especially for those fanatical Catholics—such hypocrites—who lived in the deepest and most fundamental contradiction. He liked the Bible too, and sometimes read me parts of the Book of Proverbs, or Ecclesiastes. He thought the New Testament not as good a book as the Old in literary terms, but he recognized that, morally, the Gospel was a step forward, holding out an ideal of human behaviour far more advanced than that which emerged from the more beautiful, but altogether less ethical, Pentateuch, where it was permitted to whip slaves to death for bad behaviour.

Many other things were read in our house, both pious and profane. My father sometimes bought the Spanish edition of *Reader's Digest*, and used to read me the section called 'Laughter, the best medicine,' but he skipped the bits where they denigrated Communism with sordid stories from the gulag, refusing to believe what seemed to him pure propaganda. By way of compensation, he would give me books published in the Soviet Union. I remember at least three: *The Universe is a Vast Ocean* by Valentina Tereshkova, the first female astronaut; another by Yuri Gagarin, in which the space pioneer said he'd looked out into outer space and hadn't seen God there either (which my father thought was a silly and superficial proof, since God might well be invisible); and the most important one, Aleksandr Oparin's *The Origin of Life*, which retold the story of Genesis without reference to divine intervention, and which my father explained to me paragraph by paragraph, so that I would be able to resolve my first questions about the Cosmos and the living beings in it with scientific explanations, replacing the poetic Book with its seven days of miraculous flashes of lightning and the All-powerful being who mysteriously all of a sudden grew tired as if he were a farmer, with the knowledge of a chemical Primordial Soup bombarded by stellar radiation over millions of years, until finally, by accident or necessity, the first amino acids and bacteria had appeared. I still have these books, in which I wrote my name in 1967, with the tentative handwriting of children who have only just learned how to write, and with the signature I used for all of my childhood: Héctor Abad III. I'd invented this to sign off a letter I sent my father during one of his trips to Asia, explaining it to him with these words: 'Héctor Abad III, because you're worth two.'

As a result of my conversations with my father, at school I aligned myself, at times secretly and at others publicly, with the Russians, in a hypothetical war against the Americans. Our shared faith didn't last long, since when my father was invited to travel to the Soviet Union, at the beginning of the seventies, he realized that there was a great deal of truth in the propaganda from *Reader's Digest*, and returned feeling totally disillusioned about the achievements of 'real socialism.' Above all, he was scandalized at the unbearable extent of the Police State and its unpardonable attacks on individual freedom and human rights.

'We're going to have to make a Latin American-style socialism, because the one over there is horrific,' my father said, with a certain regret at having to admit this.

He sincerely believed that the future of the world had to be socialist, if we wanted to overcome all the poverty and injustice, and until his trip to Russia, he had thought that the Soviet model might be the one to follow. This belief, not shared by my mother (who, when she had witnessed the Cuban Revolution in Havana, had told them straight out that she liked the Mexican one better), was reflected in the most simple, everyday things. For instance, when I was a year old and a pale, bald, dumpy baby, my mother and father argued about who I most looked like: she swore I was virtually identical to John XXIII, then Pope, while he claimed I was the spitting image of Nikita Khrushchev, General Secretary of the Communist Party of the Soviet Union. My mother must have won the argument, as the farm we spent the holidays at that year ended up being nicknamed Castel Gandolfo, rather than The Kremlin.

14

In response to my concerns, my father would read me bits from *Colliers Encyclopaedia*, which we had in English, or extracts from the great authors 'necessary for a liberal education,' in the words of the prologue to *Classics from the Encyclopaedia Britannica*, a collection of some fifty volumes bound in imitation leather, and containing the most important works of Western culture. On the flyleaf of each volume of the Colliers, proclaiming its faith in the benefits of scientific progress, was a timeline showing civilization's great advances, from the invention of fire and the wheel to space voyages and the computer. If I asked my father how far away the stars were, or where babies came from, or about earthquakes, dinosaurs or volcanoes, he always turned to the pages and illustrations of the *Colliers Encyclopaedia*.

He also used to show me an art book, whose importance I only realized many years later: *The Story of Art*, by Ernst Gombrich. While my father was at the university I opened this book many times, always at the same page.

Together with the huge tome of the Dictionary of the Spanish Royal Academy, where I looked up rude words, *The Story of Art* was my first encounter with pornography, and since it was in English I treated it as a magazine, looking only at the illustrations. The painting I always gazed longest at, in great emotional and physiological confusion, showed a naked woman, her pubis barely covered by a branch, breastfeeding a child while a young man observes her, a bulging shape between his legs. A flash of lightning illuminates the background, and the thunderclap from that painting was like the explosion of my erotic life. Back then I didn't care about the name of the painting or its creator, but now I know (I still have the book) that it is *The Tempest* by Giorgione, and that it was painted at the beginning of the *cinquecento*. The full, fleshy forms of that woman seemed to me the most disturbing and appealing thing I'd ever seen, possibly excepting the perfect face of my first love, a girl in my class at primary school I was never brave enough to speak to: Nelly Martínez, a little girl with angelic features who, if I'm not mistaken, was an aviator's daughter, which only made her more ethereal, mysterious and interesting in my eyes.

A period of even greater confusion began when I was taken out of the mixed primary school and moved to the secondary school where my Uncle Javier, the one from Opus Dei, was chaplain. In the unfortunate absence of girls, the only possible sources of eroticism were the bodies of my male classmates: if one of them had feminine facial features, or prominent buttocks, or walked like a girl, the most libidinous of us could not help being turned on, in an inevitable confusion of feelings and throbbing hearts.

For me school was another extreme environment, the

realm of a repressive, medieval, white and classist religion—nearly all my classmates came from the richest families in Medellín. It was a hard and masculine world, competitive, harsh and violent, and enveloped in a terrible fear of sin, an obsession with the sixth commandment (against fornication), and a morbid aversion to sex, which was drummed into us in an effort to repress at all costs the uncontrollable sensuality that seeped from our pores, fed by waves of youthful hormones.

Our teachers' crusade against sex might have been a 'mission impossible,' but it was waged with zeal. In the propaganda films we were made to watch in the school library, the Founder of Opus Dei spoke of the 'heroism of chastity.' I'll never forget that in one of these films Monsignor Escrivá de Balaguer (now made a saint by the Holy Mother Church), having extolled Franco's victory over 'the Reds' and impressed upon us with unyielding fury that most pure virtue of chastity, stared at the camera with piercing eyes and a malicious smile, as he slowly repeated: 'You don't believe in Hell? You'll see, you'll soon see.'

My uncle was replaced as chaplain by Father Mario (though we weren't allowed to call him Father, since there was only one Father and that was *The* Father, Monsignor Escrivá). Each week we had to visit him for tête-à-tête spiritual guidance interviews, which always began the same way:

'My son, how pure are you today?'

I believe he took a vicarious and unmentionable delight in these mornings and afternoons spent listening to us, as, in a long session of oral pornography, we confessed one after another the details of our irrepressible longing for sex. Father Mario always wanted details, more details: with whom, how many times, with which hand, at what time, where ... We sensed that these sins, although he condemned them, attracted him in a sick, persistent way, and so the only thing revealed by his relentless interrogations was his own eagerness.

At dusk, after those endless, dull days of school and mediocre teachers (with a couple of exceptions), I returned, after a long bus journey from Sabaneta to Laureles, to the feminine universe of my house. There too sex was concealed or denied. When we were young and all bathed together, to save hot water, in the bathtub in Dr. Saunders's room, Sister Josefa would allow my sisters to undress and reveal the curious crack between their legs shaped like the slot in a piggy bank, but she forbade me to remove my underpants, owing to the rare trinity, unique among my siblings, that sprouted from the centre of my body. My father and I showered together naked though, and he explained to my sisters with gigantic, explicit pictures how babies were made. It was left to him to right the balance when he returned from university in the evening, assuaging my worries with kindness and dedication. He contradicted my teachers, criticized the nun for her medieval, puritanical attitudes, removed Hell from the geography of the afterlife (replacing it with Terra Incognita), and reestablished order in the chaos of my thoughts. From two senseless religious passions—one masculine, at school; the other feminine, at home—I had a nocturnal, enlightened refuge: my father.

15

Why had my father, who had studied in secular State schools, given in and allowed me to be educated in a private Catholic school? I suppose his hand was forced by the undeniable decline of Colombia's state education system in the sixties and seventies. Due to badly paid and badly chosen teachers, banded together in fierce and greedy unions that allowed mediocrity and intellectual laziness to flourish, to lack of support from a state that no longer viewed publicly-funded education as a major priority (as the elite in government chose to send their children to private schools and let the people get by as best they could), to the teaching profession losing prestige and status, and the impoverishment and uncontrolled growth of the poorest sectors of the population—due to these reasons, and many others, state-funded secular schools began a process of decline from which they have yet to recover. And so, with irritated resignation, unable to deny reality, my father had let my mother, who was more practical, choose our schools: a girls' school for my sisters and a boys' school for me, and both by necessity private—which in Medellín was synonymous with religious.

She sent my sisters to the nuns of La Enseñanza and later to Marie Poussepin, where she herself had completed her secondary school certificate. And for me, after kindergarten at the girls' school and a few years at the local primary, she decided that the best thing would be to go to the school of the Society of Jesus, San Ignacio. After all, the Jesuits had had centuries of experience in educating young boys, and surely must know how to do that, at the very least.

I remember visiting the school together one afternoon to request a place, having made an appointment with the rector. After making us wait for some time, though he was obviously alone, as important businessmen usually do, the rector, Father Jorge Hoyos, received us coldly and distantly, in the manner of one trying to impose reverential respect. He was already on his feet when we entered as if not wishing his visitors to see him standing up—like the character in *The Leopard*. Without even bothering to answer her greeting, addressing my mother formally, he launched straight into an interrogation:

'Jorge, it's been ages! How are you?'

'What brings you here, Madam?'

I sensed right away that things were not going according to plan. My mother had told me before we left that it would be easy, since she and 'Jorge' had been lifelong friends, especially when they were young, before he became a Jesuit priest. But that 'Madam' indicated that she could no longer call him Jorge, and must instead address him as Father Hoyos, or even Sir. With school places limited and very sought after, the reason for our visit was clear, and he had consciously assumed the superior manner of someone with the power to grant or deny a favour.

'I am here, Father, to request a place in your school for my son, who is coming to the end of primary school.' Here she tousled my hair and told him my full name, my age, and that I was a hardworking child. Father Hoyos replied, without acknowledging me and without asking us to sit down:

'Ah, Madam, it's not as easy as you might think, no matter how good a student the child is. Look, I have three drawers here,' continued the rector, walking over to a filing cabinet and opening one drawer after another, very slowly, so we could see the piles of application letters inside. 'I call this first one Heaven, and it's for the students who get in straight away.'

My mother, seeing better than I did where things were headed, said:

'And I'm sure we're not in there ...'

'Precisely. Then there's the Purgatory drawer, this one here, where we will put your son's application—what was his name?' My mother repeated it, and he pronounced my name very slowly, syllable by syllable, with extreme sarcasm: 'Héc-tor Jo-a-quín. With these applications we must conduct a meticulous analysis of each child's family, in order to determine whether or not he should be admitted, whether perhaps in the bosom of the family there might be some sort of negative influence,'—here he opened his eyes very wide, by way of emphasizing the evil insinuation—'or even a pernicious one, from a moral or doctrinal point of view.'

He stopped for a minute, staring hard at my mother, his eyes still wide open as if to show her the image, there in his mind's eye, of the bald, bespectacled doctor who aroused so much anger throughout the city.

'And finally we have the Hell drawer, which is for those who have not even the slightest hope of coming here. Sometimes they go straight in, but sometimes they fall in, as if pulled by gravity, from the Purgatory above.'

At this point my mother could take no more, and with the distant smile she had perhaps learned when dealing with her uncle the archbishop, that offhand pleasantness that was her way of putting others in their place, she replied, with a sudden change of tone and form of address:

'Oh, Jorge, you can put us straight into the Hell drawer, because I'm going to go and find a place at some other school. Sorry to bother you. See you around.'

And with that she took my hand, as we turned and hurried out of the San Ignacio rectory, without shaking hands or looking back at the face of the priest, whom we never saw again.

16

So it was that I ended up at Los Alcázares School, 'an establishment spiritually advised by the Opus Dei,' where in spite of my father's 'pernicious ideology' I was immediately granted a place thanks to the influence of my uncle Javier. For me, this school had the advantage that two of my cousins went there, Jaime Andrés and Bernardo, who were both my age, and this made me confident of a relatively easy first few weeks as a 'new boy,' a time full of torments and tricks in any school. It seems strange that my father, who at family gatherings always argued terribly with Uncle Javier about religion (they would both lose their tempers and start shouting when they argued about the problem of Evil) simply gave in to my mother's gentle but insistent pressure. Perhaps I too insisted on being sent there, without having considered the religious aspect, and that may have been why he didn't put up a fight. Or he may have consciously resigned himself to a hopeless fate it was better not to try to resist. In the Middle Ages, monasteries had been the only places of refuge for those of a studious bent, and it was a sign of the retrograde times that in our city the only schools that could offer his son a good academic training were denominational ones. Probably it also occurred to him that 'living in opposition' might help confirm me in the beliefs he was steering me towards.

On deeper reflection, it seems to me that during those years he was prey to an inner confusion. On the one hand he was determined to educate me as a non-believer, according to the dictates of reason, and with the aim of liberating me from all the phantoms of religious repression and guilt that tormented him his whole life. But at the same time his tolerance (he would always allow all ideas to be set out in full before taking sides) and his unwillingness to contradict my mother's beliefs, led him to acknowledge that the more serious, more rigorous and more disciplined education imparted by priests might be the best, or the least bad, option. And so in the end he was unable to carry his initial line of reasoning through to its conclusion, and simply let things happen as they happened, without resisting.

There is no sense in feeling regret at something that depended so little on one's own will and so much on the circumstance of having been born at a particular historical moment, in a particular corner of the world, and into a particular home. I was lucky—it's good to look on the bright side—to be educated at Los Alcázares, in a scholastic tradition that at least respected the rigour of Aristotelian logic, and believed that faith's truths could be reached through reason, by following the intricate intellectual pathways laid by the Church's doctor, Saint Thomas Aquinas. It would have served the priests' purpose better to have sent us down the less rational, more slippery path of Saint Augustine, a thinker far harder to refute, since he appealed not to reason but to impulse. But we were made to read even the most obscure and difficult authors of the Thomist school: *The Criterion* by Balmes, the twisted thoughts of Monsignor Escrivá de Balaguer, as well as the Spanish Falange's diatribes against atheist materialism, modern secularism and things like that.

At the same time, my father concocted his home-made antidotes to the education I was getting, countering my school reading, impregnated with Catholic patristics and philosophy, with other books and other ideas, far more convincing to me. If in Religion or Science they glossed over evolutionary theory (or claimed that it hadn't been proved beyond doubt), or in Philosophy they skipped quickly through Voltaire, D'Alembert and Diderot, I could always vaccinate myself in my father's study with small doses of these very men, immunizing me against their destruction—or with Nietzsche and Schopenhauer, Darwin or Huxley. Against Leibniz and Saint Thomas' proofs of the existence of God there was the antibiotic of Kant or Hume (who strongly criticized miracles), the more accessible and playful scepticism of Borges, and above all the refreshing clarity of the great Bertrand Russell, who was my father's philosophical idol, and the liberator of my young mind.

Ultimately, faith or the lack of it does not depend on our will, or on any mysterious grace received from on high, but on those lessons we learn early on, one way or another, and which are almost impossible to unlearn. If in infancy and early youth we are instilled with metaphysical beliefs, or on the contrary are taught an agnostic or atheist point of view, when we reach adulthood we will find ourselves all but incapable of changing our position. Children are programmed to believe uncritically what their elders tell them. This is a good thing: just imagine what the world would be like if we were born sceptics and, in a spirit of enquiry, crossed the road without looking, tested knife blades on our faces to see if they really cut, or ventured into the jungle alone. As children, blind belief in what our parents tell us is a question of survival, both in the practical sphere and in the domain of religious belief. Those who believe in ghosts or in people possessed by the devil do so not because they really see these things themselves, but because they were made to hear and see them—even if at first they couldn't—as children.

Some people, intoxicated with reason, reconsider their position when they grow up and for a few years maintain a sceptical point of view, even though they have been religiously educated. But when they are faced with life's frailties, with old age or illness, they become tremendously susceptible to faith in some sort of spiritual power. Only those in whom the seeds of doubt have been planted very early, are really able to doubt their own beliefs.

There is an additional difficulty for those who do not acknowledge the existence of a spiritual realm. Human-kind's existential agony, its overwhelming, tortured awareness of death, is such that belief in an immortal soul, able to go to Heaven or transmigrate, will always be more attractive, and more conducive to social harmony and brotherhood among distant peoples, than a cold disbelief in the supernatural. Men naturally feel a deep, passionate attraction to mystery, and it is a daily labour to avoid the temptation to believe in a metaphysical dimension, in souls that live on after physical death, and whose existence can never be proved. For if the soul and the mind are one and the same, all it takes is a brain injury or the dark abysses of Alzheimer's disease to show that the soul, as a philosopher once said, is not only not immortal, but far more mortal even than the body.

17

During my childhood and teenage years, in the sixties and seventies, my father had frequent ideological clashes with the university's board of governors. Of course I didn't directly witness these clashes; but the conversations my mother and father would have in the dining room and the bedroom were tense and interminable. She firmly supported him in everything, helped him to bear the most unjust persecutions and suggested diplomatic survival strategies. But a time came when my father had no choice but to go away on long journeys, journeys incomprehensible to me and with very painful consequences, which I was only able to make sense of years later.

During those decades he endured the constant persecution of Conservatives, by whom he was considered left-wing in politics and free-thinking in religion— a harmful influence on students and a danger to society. Towards the end of the seventies, he had to put up with reverse McCarthyism, and the savage jokes and incessant criticism of the left-wingers who had replaced the Conservatives in some college posts, and who regarded him as a half-hearted and incorrigible bourgeois because of his opposition to the armed struggle. During the transition period, while the left were replacing the right in the university, my father advocated ideological tolerance more than ever, and what he termed 'mesoism,' meaning moderation and negotiation. I remember him repeating often this phrase (I don't recall whether he was quoting someone else): 'Those whom the Ghibellines accuse of being Guelphs, and whom the Guelphs accuse of being Ghibellines—they are the ones who are right.'

He found it grotesque when the Marxists converted the old chapel on the university campus first into a laboratory, then into a theatre. Although my father believed that the university ought to be a secular institution, he saw it not as a renunciation of the secular ideal to respect a place of worship (especially when most of the professors and students were still believers) but as the expression of a liberal creed that tolerated all the intellectual manifestations of man, including the religious. And he would have seen no harm in the university accommodating a Buddhist temple, a synagogue, a mosque and a Masonic chapel. To him the fundamentalism of non-believers was just as pernicious as that of those who had faith.

But in the early sixties, when I was barely three or four years old, the fight was with the representatives of the far right, as it would be again in the eighties. In about 1961 the first serious conflict broke out between my father and those who at that time were in the highest ranks of the University of Antioquia, his Alma Mater and where he worked as a professor, in spite of everything, until the last day of his life. The rector, Jaime Sanín Echeverri, who was of a Conservative bent (though the years filed down his sharpest edges and he reached a less fanatical old age), and the Dean of Medicine, Oriol Arango, began to persecute him, openly aiming to force him to resign his chair. At one point there was a teachers' strike and my father supported it with articles and appearances on the radio and in the square. As a result he received this letter of reprimand from the Dean, Dr. Arango:

'Sir: when I assumed the post of Dean, you and I agreed it was necessary to free the Professorship of Preventative Medicine, for the good of the faculty, from what you referred to as 'ill will' and I as the stigma of Communism. I was grateful for your promise not to spare any effort in this necessary campaign. But I have now received numerous reports about the part you played on the public stage and on the radio, participating in a recent movement that degenerated into an illegal strike. In such cases we wonder whether you are using your professorship purely to carry out university work, or attempting to stir up unrest among the masses. Your attitude is not compatible with the post of University Professor and the moment has come for you to define your position and choose between devoting yourself entirely to teaching or to other activities.'

My father's reply, after informing the Dean of certain projects he was undertaking in a village near Medellín with an American philanthropist (he was referring to Dr. Saunders)—effective, useful and real Public Health practice—contained the following reflections:

'Sir: I must make it clear to you, with all due respect, that I have never understood my professorial position as requiring the renunciation of my civil rights or the free expression of my ideas and opinions as I see fit. In the five years I have been a professor on this faculty, this is the first time an attempt has been made to forbid me from exercising these rights. Under the two previous deans I wrote to the press and expressed my views on the radio, and while it is possible that this caused 'ill will' (in certain corners) towards this professorship, I do not regret having done so in the slightest, since I believe I have always had the public good in mind. Moreover, I believe that the position I hold is essentially one of general service to Colombian society, requiring contact with Colombian reality: it would not be possible for me to isolate myself or the students in an academic ivory tower. On the contrary, we must connect fully with real Colombian problems, not only those of the future or the past, but of the present too, so that the university does not remain an ethereal entity, remote from the people's distress, ignoring half the population as it persists with the outdated practices and privileges that have kept the Colombian people in the Dark Ages, when it comes to social justice.

'Only yesterday, riding with the director of an American social work association, I visited some agricultural *slave*-labourers, who have no water, no land, no hope. On my return I was planning to tell my students and the general public about this, and invite them to go and meet these labourers so that together we might come up with better ways to remedy such lamentable circumstances. If these ideas are incompatible with the professorship, you may resolve the situation as you deem appropriate, sir, but I do not plan to renounce them because of any economic or political pressure, or to abandon them regretfully, having spent my whole life fighting for them and for my right to express them.'

This time the reply came not from the Dean, but from

the university's board of governors. The rector, all the deans of faculty, along with representatives of the president, of the minister for education, of the professors, of the former rectors, and of the students, unanimously supported Dr. Arango's position. My father wrote a vigorous reply, but understood he was being squeezed out of the university, and that they were all watching him like hawks for the slightest pretext to dismiss him.

It was then, around 1963 or '64, when my father began to request lengthy periods of leave, hoping to avoid the rough weather, like aviators who fly around the anvil-shaped storm clouds in their way to rejoin the established flight path further on. In his first few years as a doctor he had worked in Washington, Lima and Mexico as a consultant for the World Health Organization, and was able to secure various international medical consultancies, first in Indonesia and Singapore, then in Malaysia and the Philippines. He was always granted leave immediately by the board, happy for some temporary relief from the headache personified by this rebellious doctor.

These intervals of absence were not enough to still the waters. When he returned he found that his former students (whom he had protected, recommended and appointed) would greet him with stones in their hands. One in particular, Guillermo Restrepo Chavarriaga, insulted him and accused him of being 'a demagogue with the student body and dictator with the teaching staff,' as well as of professing 'a dangerous philosophy in conflict with the progress of the School and health.' These accusations always took my father by surprise, and he would read these letters in near disbelief. They were trying to kick him out of the very School of Public Health he had founded and headed. After a time he would feel obliged to seek another international consultancy, so he could continue to support his family without being humiliated at the university.

His trips could last for more than six months, and the first few days of his absence were like a living death for me. I would beg my mother to let me sleep in his bed, asking the maids not to change the sheets or pillowcases, so I could still sleep with my father's smell. And they did as I asked, at least until my own body and the passing of time had erased that wonderful scent, which I had only to inhale to feel calm and protected.

In those days a phone call from the other side of the world cost a small fortune, and my father could only afford a very short call, once a month, in which it was impossible to talk to all six children and my mother. So he would speak to her for five minutes, and she, shouting over the whistles and murmurs of the ether, had to tell him, in a jumbled rush, how we all were, one by one, and what news there was in the family and the country. Of course there were the letters every week: he wrote often to the family and to each of us individually. We wrote to him too, and the filing cabinet in the house still contains some of his replies, always loving and affectionate, full of reflections and advice for each one of us, tempering the pain of separation with memories and their reminder of the constancy of his love for us. I would return desolately to my bedroom, putting his postcards and letters under the mattress. They kept me company at night and were my secret aid to sleep, those strings of words that brought my father's voice to me all the way from Asia.

These letters, and the memory of hundreds and hundreds of conversations I had with him, have helped me realize that, though we are not born good, if someone tolerates and directs our innate meanness, we may be guided down less harmful channels, or even led to change direction altogether. We do not have to learn to take revenge (we are born with vengeful feelings), but not to take revenge. We must be taught not so much to be good, as not to be bad. I have never felt like a good person, but I think that, thanks to my father's influence, I have sometimes managed to be a non-practising bad man, a coward who with effort overcomes his cowardice and a miser who controls his avarice. Most importantly, if there is any happiness in my life, if I am at all grown-up, if most of the time I behave in a decent and more or less normal fashion, if I'm not antisocial and have peacefully endured attacks and hardships, I believe it is simply because my father loved me just as I was, an amorphous bundle of good and bad feelings, and showed me how to get the best from this bad human nature, which perhaps we all share. And although I don't always achieve it, in his memory I almost always try to be less bad than I am prompted to be by my natural inclinations.

18

The problem was that when he went away for months and months, I was defenceless against the dark Catholicism of my mother's family. Several nights a week I had to go to Grandma Victoria's house. She was the youngest of seven, born in Bucaramanga after a string of six brothers, and got her name from the exclamation of my great-grandfather, José Joaquín, upon her entrance into the world: 'Victory at last!'

My grandmother was surrounded by devout men. Among her brothers she counted an archbishop (Joaquín) and a monsignor (Luis García); another brother, Jesús García, had married yet ultimately was more of a priest than the other two, (attending Mass three times a day, and devoting his life after his wife died to the twin passions of religion and reminding everyone that he had been Minister of Post Offices and Telegraphs during Abadía Méndez's government, until the disastrous coming to power of the Liberals, Masons and radicals), and Alberto was Colombian consul in Havana (a little livelier than his brothers, perhaps the least bible-bashing of the family). She was also the aunt of Joaquín García Ordóñez, bishop of Santa Rosa de Osos, as well as of the two rebel priests I've already mentioned, René García and Luis Alejandro Currea.

Outside her devout and masculine family, her social life was no less Catholic. Her confessors and close friends included Monsignor Uribe, who would become bishop of Rionegro and the most famous exorcist in Colombia, Father Lisandeo Franky, parish priest in Aracataca, and Father Tisnés, historian of the Academy. These Levitical connections made her the natural hostess of the Apostolic Sewing Circle, a group of women who met every Wednesday afternoon from two until six, and tirelessly sewed the vestments of the city's priests, which they gave away free to the poor ones and sold for a fortune to the rich. They sewed, knitted and embroidered albs, cinctures, stoles, chasubles, amices for covering the back, purifiers for the altar, cloths to polish the ciborium, and surplices for the seminarians and altar boys.

My grandmother's house smelled of incense, like a cathedral, and was crowded with motley statues and images of saints, like a pagan temple: the Sacred Heart of Jesus, his entrails showing; Saint Anne, teaching the Holy Virgin to read; Saint Anthony of Padua, preaching to the birds with his uncorrupted tongue; Saint Martin of Porres protecting the black people of Peru; the *Curé d'Ars*, Saint John Vianney, on his deathbed. A series of immense photos of the late archbishop, eyes hidden by his blind man's dark glasses, hung on the dining room walls and in the long, dark corridors, along with several letters framed in gold-leaf because they bore the signature of Cardinal Pacelli, later His Holiness Pius XII after the Holy Spirit named him Pope shortly before the Second World War, to the misfortune of the Jews and the shame of Christianity. As well as these sacred objects and devotions and images, the house was filled with the permanent scent of the sacristy and of burning candles, fear of sin, and convent gossip.

The house had a chapel and an oratory, and as evening fell, my sisters and I would all sit around Grandmother in the oratory, and women would begin to emerge from every corner of the house: women relatives and women servants and women neighbours, women always dressed in black or dark brown, like cockroaches, mantillas on their heads and rosary beads in hand. The rosary ceremony was presided over by Uncle Luis with his glossy old cassock, stained with ash and worn out with ironing, with his raw leper's hands and the tonsure on the white crown of his head. He looked like a giant, at once smiling and furious, both scandalized and in despair at the commonplace sins and incorrigible sinners he had to absolve every evening in the confessional of his apartment. He would wait patiently, smoking one cigarette after another and singeing his fingers, repeating over and over his old despairing chant ('Oh, when, when will we get to Heaven!'), until all the women had arrived, from indoors and out.

There was Marta Castro, who'd been consumptive and had been left with a dry, muted, permanent cough and quick, anxious breathing, and who also had one cloudy, bluish-grey eye, because once while embroidering a chasuble she had pricked her retina with a needle, and had lost her sight in that eye—that was how God had repaid her for doing charitable work for the poor priests. Just as He had repaid Uncle Luis himself, who had gone to be a chaplain in Agua de Dios, Colombia's leper colony in Cundinamarca, and contracted the disease that would kill him, his back peeling away bit by bit, his fingers coming off in pieces. Once, near the end of his days, my grandmother was making his bed when suddenly, on the sheet, all by itself, she saw his big toe. She ran to call the doctor, but it was already too late, because as well as Hansen's disease he had developed diabetes, and they had to amputate his legs, first one then the other. Later, believe it or not, this also happened to Father Lisandro, my grandma's confessor, whose legs had to be amputated after they became gangrenous due to poor circulation caused by diabetes. Both had been struck down from on high as punishment for their devotion, Christian zeal and apostolic celibacy. Well before the amputation of his legs, the virus had seen to Uncle Luis's fingers, eating them away and leaving him with those terrible stumps through which he passed the rosary beads.

And there was Tatá too, of course, first my grandmother's nanny and then my mother's, who lived for six months in our house and six in Grandma's house, and who was completely deaf. She would say the rosary to her own rhythm, and while we intoned 'Holy Mary, Mother of God, pray for us sinners, now and at the hour of death, Amen,' she would tunelessly be chanting, 'Hail Mary, full of grace, the Lord is with thee; blessed art thou among women, and blessed is the fruit of thy womb ...' Something awful happened to Tatá too, later on, after the best eye surgeon in Medellín, Dr. Alberto Llano operated on her cataracts. Back then the operation was done with a scalpel rather than a laser and the wound was a large one, so she wasn't allowed to get out of bed or lift her head up for two months—two months of total stillness while my mother looked after her, washing her with a flannel. One morning, while my mother was helping her change her pyjamas, Tatá raised her head, and as she did so her eye began to empty itself out. A gelatinous substance, like raw egg white, dripped from the socket, and my mother was left with a putrid-smelling jelly and Tatá's eye in her hand (just as earlier my grandmother had held Uncle Luis's gangrenous big toe in hers). So Tatá lost her sight forever in that eye, and with the other she could barely see a thing, only light and shadows, or very large objects, as shapes. She didn't dare have another operation to remove the cataracts from this remaining eye, and to communicate with her my mother bought a classroom style blackboard and some chalk, and anything you wanted to say to her you had to write on the board in immense letters. Tatá prayed and prayed constantly, because these were things sent by God to test us or to make us suffer here on Earth, in advance, some of the torments of Purgatory, so necessary to cleanse the soul before we could become worthy of Heaven.

Sometimes Blondie Jack came too. He had got throat cancer from smoking and praying, and they had removed his larynx, so he had almost no voice, speaking in a peculiar gargling that came from his stomach. My sisters and I were told that he breathed, like a whale, through his back, where they had made him a little hole that went straight to his lungs. When he said the rosary the only sound you could hear was a nasal gurgling stuck in the throat he no longer had, and which he covered with a red silk neckerchief tied very elegantly. My sisters and I would stare in terror at the back of his shirt, watching how it swelled up with each exhalation and shrunk every time he breathed in, as if he were a dolphin. Blondie Jack owned a plot where the best guavas in the city grew, huge ones, and sometimes he invited me to climb the trees and pick them, so that at home or in Aunt Mona's house we could make guava jelly and guava pudding and guava jam and guava delight and guava juice. What most fascinated me about Blondie Jack's house was that he kept a referee's whistle hanging round his neck on a little chain, which he would blow very loudly when he wanted to call his wife, and she would answer from inside the house: 'I'm coming, Blondie, I'm coming.' But I never understood why he didn't put the whistle to his breathing hole, where a jet of air must presumably come out, as from the back of a humpback whale.

These rosaries were awful, like a procession of ruinous parishioners, like a court of miracles, like a scene from a film about Holy Week when the sick and the crippled, the blind and the lepers come to Christ so he can cure them. There was even an adulteress who came, a real sinner, a distant relative, a disgraced and nameless woman, lost forever as she had left her husband and children, and had run off to a cattle farm near Montería with another man, until he turned his back on her. And so she'd ended up with nothing, no bread and no cheese, the women said, and she had come back, but no one welcomed her and the only thing she could do was pray and say rosaries for the rest of her life in the hope that one day God would take pity on her, and forgive her for the abominable act she had had the audacity to commit. She had to sit at the back, right at the back with the maids, her head bowed, showing humility, and the other women barely looked at her; they greeted her from afar with a slight movement of their eyebrows, never inviting her to the Apostolic Sewing Circle, as if afraid that the sin she had committed might be contagious, more contagious than leprosy, flu and tuberculosis.

Also present were Rosario, who made communion wafers and sponge fingers, and Martina the ironing lady, who smelled of paste. There was Martina's daughter Marielena, too, who was mentally retarded and had a harelip, and had had three babies by three different men, because macho men don't care whether they sleep with a genius or an imbecile, they always want to stick it somewhere, any hot, fragrant hole will do. Martina had got fed up with her daughter's going off with horny men, and had taken the children away and given them up for adoption to some Canadians, as she worried that Marielena would soon get pregnant again, and what did she want so many grandchildren for? But Marielena didn't get pregnant again, and now they only saw the children on the Christmas cards that arrived in December: little Canadian children surrounded by snow and wellbeing, someone else's children who had grown pale with the cold. The cards had no return address, just 'Merry Christmas,' and Canadian stamps with the picture of the Queen of England and a Vancouver postmark, which showed which country and city it was, but not the house where the children now lived like kings, while Martina and her daughter stagnated here, alone and poor, getting older and lonelier every day. Marielena had had her tubes tied after her last dalliance and was sterile forever, so the two of them were left alone and would continue darning and ironing alone and starching tablecloths and linen napkins alone and for no one for as long as their fingers and eyes held out.

There were also 'the girls,' that's what my grandma called them, the girls from the Apostolic Sewing Circle, although they were all old ladies, even the young ones. All very old. Among them were Gertrudis Hoyos; Libia Isaza de Hernández (the inventor of Peña Pomade, who'd made a fortune from this cream that erased marks on the hands and face as if by magic, the only rich woman in the Sewing Circle and the one who gave the most money for charitable works); Alicia and Maruja Villegas, two very short and very conservative old ladies; Rocío and Luz Jaramillo; Aunt Inés, my father's sister, and my other grandmother, Doña Eva, who was always laughing hysterically for some unknown reason; Salía de Hernández, the tailor's cutter; also Margarita Fernández de Mira, the psychiatrist's mother, and Eugenia Fernández and Martina Marulanda; not forgetting Father Marulanda's sister, and more and more women who came to my grandmother's house to sew and gossip and say the rosary with Uncle Luis, Monsignor García—my poor uncle sick with leprosy, who everyone steered clear of, although no one would ever say the word or mention this disease, not my mother, or my grandmother, or the maids, or the old girls in the Apostolic Sewing Circle, or anyone, they said only 'his trial,' or 'his trouble'—the trial and trouble that God had sent in return for saying so many rosaries for Him, for taking communion so many times, for confessing every week and saying Mass and Mass and Mass again, imploring Him for miracles that never arrived, and for mercy, which always came disguised as suffering, tragedy and misfortune.

My mother never attended these sewing circles and hardly ever the rosary sessions, because she worked and was a practical woman, with few friends, who detested the perpetual gossip at the gatherings, and the permanent smell of priests and sacristy, which was the smell of her childhood. She offloaded us all there, my sisters and me, partly to be looked after, but also, I think, so that we'd have a little taste of her own childhood, having to say the rosary there with all those old women. We would feel what her fatherless childhood had been like in that house that oozed Catholicism: prayers, pious women, saints and sinners, human deformities, public and secret tragedies, embarrassing diseases, in that devotional house that God had chosen to smite, just like any other house, like all the houses on this Earth, with his fury, represented by a heavy dose of misery, absurd deaths, incurable pains and diseases.

19

So, when my father went on leave for months to Jakarta, Manila, Kuala Lumpur and, years later, to Los Angeles, where he was invited to give classes in Public Health at the University of California (and later turned up at our house with his American students, with Allan and Terry and Keith and others I don't remember, and I'd have to share a bedroom with these huge, blonde gringos who had come to see the miseries of the tropics, me without a word of English, or with my one and only phrase, *it stinks, it stinks, it stinks*, which at times was nothing but the truth since it was into the toilet in *my* room that they would vomit, sick as dogs, when—to take one example—my mum happened to have the stupendous idea of serving for lunch that great delicacy of a whole stewed ox tongue, enormous, red and slimy, cooked to Doña Jesusita's recipe and laid out on a silver platter like the head of Saint John the Baptist, or Holofernes), when my father went to all these places for months on end I was left at the mercy of these Catholicism-afflicted women, which meant at the mercy of my Grandma Victoria too. And while it can't be denied she could be gentle and cheerful, at least when she wasn't praying, especially with my sisters (with whom she talked about love and boyfriends), when I got back after school, it was the hour of devotion and the Holy Rosary with Uncle Luis, and to me this was Hell on earth—no matter how many times we were told at the start that 'the Mysteries we are going to meditate on today are the joyful ones,' among them Mary's visit to her cousin Saint Elizabeth and also the loss and discovery in the temple of the child Jesus, which was how I felt, a child lost in the temple of my grandmother's house, with no father to rescue me. On other days we meditated on the so called 'glorious mysteries,' such as the passing of Mary from this earthly life to the eternal one, and the resurrection of Our Lord Jesus Christ. But the mysteries I recall most clearly, those best suited to my state of mind, were the sorrowful ones: the five thousand and more lashes, the heavy cross put on His delicate shoulders, the crown of thorns, the prayer in the garden, the sacrificial death on the cross. We would scarcely have finished meditating on these Roman tortures when the eternal litanies of Loreto to the Most Holy Virgin began. These were said at the end in Latin (perhaps the first foreign language I heard, the language of empire and rites) until the Second Vatican Council removed it. It was an endless, soothing, rhythmic chant that went something like this: *Sancta Maria, ora pro nobis, Mater purissima, ora pro nobis, Mater castissima, ora pro nobis, Mater inviolata, ora pro nobis, Mater intemerata, ora pro nobis, Mater amabilis, ora pro nobis, Mater admirabilis, ora pro nobis, Virgo prudentissima, ora pro nobis, Virgo veneranda, ora pro nobis, Virgo predicanda, ora pro nobis, Virgo potens, ora pro nobis, Speculum justitiae, ora pro nobis, Turris Davidica, ora pro nobis, Turris eburnea, ora pro nobis, Causa nostra laetitia, ora pro nobis,* and more epithets, more titles and entreaties, in an insistent rhythm that seemed somehow to calm all the women present, especially the maids who could at last take a rest from work, be still for a while and sink into their own dream worlds as they repeated this completely meaningless phrase, *ora pro nobis, ora pro nobis, ora pro nobis,* this incessant repetition that, depending on the day, made me feel amused, anxious, sleepy or lazy, never spiritually elevated, and almost always unavoidably and utterly bored.

I remember the sensation I would have in the airport before seeing my father again after one of his trips that seemed to me to last for years (I found out later that I had been orphaned for a total of fifteen or twenty months, spread out over several different stages). It was a feeling of fear mixed with euphoria. It was like the agitation you feel before seeing the sea, when you can smell how close it is, and even hear the far-off roar of the waves, but you can't yet see it, only sense, intuit and imagine it. I see myself on the balcony of Olaya Herrera Airport, a large terrace with a window overlooking the runway, my knees pushed between the bars, my arms almost touching the airplanes' wings, and the announcement over the loudspeakers, 'Flight HK-2142 from Panama is about to land,' followed by the distant roar of the engines, the sight of the aluminium as it approached us, gleaming in the sun, heavy, dense, majestic, coming round the side of Nutibara Hill, grazing the summit with a tragic, dizzying proximity. Finally the Super Constellation carrying my father landed, a formidable whale that took the entire length of the runway to come to a halt at last in the final few metres, then slowly turned and approached the platform, slow as an ocean liner about to dock, too slow for my nerves (I had to jump up and down on the spot to contain them). Then it turned off its four propeller engines that took an age to stop spinning, the invisible blades forming a fog of liquid air, and they wouldn't open the door until they'd completely stopped, while the airport workers pushed and adjusted the white steps. I stood with my sisters, all dressed up in little lace skirts, and my breathing grew agitated as a line of people began to emerge from the plane's belly, through the door at the front. That's not him, that's not him, that's not him, or that, until finally, right at the top of the steps, he appeared, unmistakable, with his dark suit, his tie, his shiny bald head, his thick square-framed glasses and his happy face, waving at us from a distance, smiling from up high, our hero, the father returning from a mission in deepest Asia, laden with gifts (pearls and Chinese silks, little marble and ebony sculptures, teak chests filled with tablecloths and cutlery, Balinese dancers, peacock-feather fans, Indian fabrics with tiny mirrors and sea shells, tablets of aromatic incense), with laughter, with stories, with joy, to rescue me from that sordid world of rosaries, diseases, sins, skirts and soutanes, prayers, spirits, phantoms and superstition. Rarely have I felt such relief and happiness, for here came my saviour, my one true Saviour.

20

Though my parents' beliefs were contradictory, they complemented each other well, and in their day-to-day life were loving and affectionate. Yet as a child I experienced the radical difference between my two role models, the contrast of attitudes, character and education, as an intractable riddle. He was agnostic and she almost mystical; he hated money and she poverty; he was a materialist when it came to the afterlife and spiritual in earthly matters, while she left spiritualism for the afterlife and pursued material goods here on earth. These differences seemed to draw them together rather than push them apart, perhaps because they shared a deep core of ethical beliefs about which they agreed completely. My father consulted my mother about everything, and she was able to see things through his eyes, offering him a deep, unconditional love that was immune to all setbacks, to radical disagreement of any kind, or the pernicious information about him she received from time to time from his detractors, pretending to have her interests at heart.

'I love him as he is, all of him, with all his qualities and all his defects, and I even like the things about him I don't agree with,' my mother told us many times.

As soon as they saw each other, no matter how long or short the time since they had last spoken, and at whatever time of day, even first thing in the morning, they would launch into an account of everything that had happened to them (including daydreams and nightmares) with the enthusiasm of friends who hadn't seen each other for weeks. They told each other about the good and bad experiences of the day and chatted non-stop about every topic: their children's lives, work problems, the little triumphs and defeats of daily life. When they were apart, they always spoke well of each other, and each independently taught us to love their partner's different qualities. Sometimes in the morning, mainly at the farm at Rionegro, I would find them cuddling in bed, talking. My father wrote her poems and love songs (which his children had to recite and sing), comic couplets for every birthday, and the same sentimental song every anniversary, which my sister Marta accompanied on the guitar ('without you, I'd be a shadow, I'd be nothing without your love ...'). Towards the end of his life my father even started to grow roses on the farm; the reason, as he explained in an interview, was simple: 'Why roses? Because my wife, Cecilia, really likes roses.' In turn, my mother worked very hard, essentially for an altruistic reason: so that my father wouldn't have to worry about earning money, so that he could give it away, as he liked to do, without worrying that he was neglecting his family, but above all so he could maintain his intellectual independence in the university, so they couldn't shut him up, as is so common in this country, with the threat and pressure of poverty.

I've already discussed my father's attraction to the values of the Enlightenment, and his theological agnosticism. My mother, on the other hand, was and still is mystical, although she is always wishing she had 'much more faith.' She is a believer, a strong believer even, a daily-Mass Catholic, as they say here, and is constantly mentioning God and the Most Holy Virgin. Her religiosity, however, had a very strong animistic, almost pagan, component, since the saints she believed in most were not those of the calendar but the souls of dead people from her own family, whom she automatically sanctified from the moment of their death, without waiting for any sort of confirmation or authorization from the Church. If she lost a banknote, or couldn't find her keys, or if one of us got sick, she would commend the matter to the soul of Uncle Joaquín, the archbishop; or, after she died, to Tatá's soul or to that of Marta Cecilia, my sister, when she died; or to her mother's, when Grandma Victoria died; or, eventually, to my father's, after he was killed. But while she was always attentive to these incorporeal otherworldly presences, my mother has never been one of those people who, as they say, 'turn their back on the world.'

On the contrary, she was—and still is—the greatest realist I have ever known, with her feet firmly planted on the ground. She managed the family budget with a firm and steady hand (always faithful to that most un-Christian principle that 'charity begins at home'), and was much better than my father at resolving the practical problems of her immediate family, as well as those of other people, if she had enough time. For my father, beginning one's charity at home wasn't being generous, but simply obeying one's most natural and primal instincts, (and not to do so was for him the same as that degenerate mental state called avarice). He believed charity meant looking beyond our immediate circle, which might explain why he was always lending or giving away his money to strangers, or donating his time to idealistic projects—which is not to say that they were not practical, like teaching poor people how to boil water, build latrines and aqueducts and sewage systems.

But my father's charity, which was boundless when it came to society as a whole, was more theoretical than practical when it came to everyday life and individuals. If a labourer came to the farm to consult him about some pain or illness, it was my mother who had to go out and see to him. It was she who listened to the symptoms, pretending to relate them to my father, while he stayed in his room reading, or kneeling among his rosebushes, as she performed the pantomime of consulting him, but in fact prescribing the patient's medicine herself. If one of them asked why he couldn't see 'the doctor' in person, my mother said it was just the same, as she had lots of practice (she passed herself off as a nurse although all she could do was apply Mercurochrome, change bandages, wash thermometers and give injections), and that she was following her husband's instructions 'to the letter.'

My father never liked practising medicine directly, and this went back, as far as I was able to reconstruct much later, to a sort of early trauma he had experienced thanks to a professor of surgery at the university. This professor had asked him to remove a patient's gallbladder before he'd had enough experience, and during the cholecystectomy, a delicate operation, he'd damaged the patient's bile duct. This patient, a young man, around forty years old, had died a few days after the operation, and what's more, when they closed him up it was already clear he would die shortly afterwards. My father was always very clumsy with his hands. He was too intellectual to be a doctor, and entirely lacked the butcher's skills needed by a surgeon. Even changing a light bulb was extremely difficult for him, not to mention changing a tyre (he used to joke that when he got a flat, he had to stand and wait on the hard shoulder, like a woman, for a man to come and rescue him) or checking a carburettor (whatever that was) or extracting a gallbladder without touching the delicate tubes surrounding it. He didn't understand mechanics and, having learned to drive late, only knew how to operate an automatic car. All his life, every time he had to perform the heroic act of entering a roundabout in the midst of traffic, he did so with his eyes shut, and used to say, every time he got behind the wheel, that he felt 'deeply nostalgic for the bus.' He wasn't agile or good at any sport, and he was completely useless in the kitchen, incapable of making himself a coffee or a boiled egg. He hated us to run risks and I was the only boy in the neighbourhood who rode a bike with a helmet (which he made me wear) and also the only one who couldn't climb trees, since my father would only let me climb the dwarf *totumo* tree in our front garden, and the biggest act of heroism I was allowed to attempt was to jump off the lowest branch, which was at most thirty centimetres off the ground.

After the man died as a result of his surgery, if I'm not mistaken, my father gave up practising his profession directly all together. He felt neither confident nor competent, and opted instead for the more general areas of medical science: hygiene, public health, epidemiology and preventative or social medicine. He practised medicine from a wholly scientific point of view, but without direct contact with patients and disease (he preferred to prevent it, with endless vaccination programmes or by teaching basic hygiene). Maybe this was partly due to an excessive sensitivity that meant he loathed blood, wounds, pus, pustules, pain, entrails, fluids, emissions and everything that is inherent to the everyday practice of medicine in direct contact with ill people.

My father, who, depending on the day, was an agnostic, a believer in the humane teachings of Jesus, a terrestrial atheist (on board planes he temporarily converted and crossed himself at the start of the flight), or a convinced atheist of the sort who would laugh at priests and give scientific and enlightened explanations of the most absurd religious superstitions, was, on the other hand, a man tormented by his moral and spiritual life. He was prey to great bursts of idealism, during which he devoted years to lost causes, such as agrarian reform or land taxes, drinkable water for all, universal vaccination, or human rights, which was his final intellectual passion and the one that led to his ultimate sacrifice. He would sink into pits of rage and indignation at social injustice, and spent his life grappling with important issues—those removed from everyday life and concerned instead with the transformation of society.

He was easily moved to tears, and was carried away by poetry and music, even religious music, with an aesthetic elevation bordering on mystical ecstasy. It was music, which he listened to shut up in his study, at full blast, that was the best medicine for him in his moments of despair and disappointment. At the same time he was a sensualist, a lover of beauty (in men and women, in nature and in the works of man), yet also oblivious to the material comforts of the world. His generosity matched that of some Christian missionaries, and seemed to have no limits, or was limited only by his not wanting to touch pain with his own hands ('I don't want to see it, I don't want to see it,' he'd chant). For him the material world seemed almost not to exist, except insofar as it was needed to fulfil the minimal conditions of subsistence with which he was obsessed, which were indispensable to all human beings and should be offered to everyone so all could devote themselves to what was truly important, to the sublime creation of knowledge, to the sciences, the arts and spiritual enlightenment. To him the discoveries and advances of science were just as incredible and beautiful as great works of music and literature. His visual, or pictorial, learning was not vast, but I clearly remember the passion with which he read to me, translating as he went, Gombrich's *The Story of Art*, that book we loved for different reasons: I because of its erotic fascination, and he because of its virtuous clarity (which I too discovered later), that of a mind at once geometric, ordered and precise, yet also able to transmit with simplicity and passion the aesthetic delights of art.

His reading was multifarious and disorderly. Most of his thousands of books, which I still have, are full of underlinings and notes, but almost never further than the first hundred or hundred and fifty pages, as if he had been suddenly seized by some sort of disappointment or disillusion, or, more likely, because another interest had usurped the previous one. He read few novels, but many books of poetry, in English, French and Spanish. He believed sincerely in Colombian poetry, and repeated almost weekly that the best poet in the country was Carlos Castro Saavedra. He seldom explained that Castro was also his best friend, and that he spent many a Saturday night with him on his farm in Rionegro next to ours, talking and drinking a few glasses of flavoured *aguardiente*. 'I drink very little because I like it a lot,' he commented when he came back from one of his evenings with Carlos, which never went on later than eleven o'clock.

He was interested in political philosophy and sociology (Machiavelli, Marx, Hobbes, Rousseau, Veblen), the exact sciences (Russell, Monod, Huxley, Darwin), philosophy (he was enamoured of Plato's *Dialogues*, which he liked to read aloud, and Voltaire's rational novels), but he jumped from one to another in an improvised, amateur fashion, and perhaps for this very reason very happily. One month he was in love with Shakespeare, the next with Antonio Machado or Lorca, and then later he couldn't put down Whitman or Tolstoy for weeks. He was a highly enthusiastic man, entranced by passions that were short-lived, perhaps due to the very intensity with which he devoted himself to them at the start, impossible to sustain for more than two or three fanatical months.

Despite all his intellectual struggles, and the deliberate search for an enlightened and tolerant liberalism, my father knew he was a victim and an involuntary representative of the prejudices of the dismal, antiquated and stagnant education he'd received in the remote villages where he grew up. 'I was born in the eighteenth century: I'm nearly two hundred years old,' he would say, remembering his childhood. Although rationally he rejected racism, arguing against it furiously (with the exaggerated passion of those who fear the spectre of its opposite and in their excess reveal that they're trying to convince themselves more than anyone else), in real life he found it hard to accept it calmly when one of my sisters went out with someone with a little more melanin than us, and sometimes he forgot himself and spoke proudly of his grandfather's blue eyes, or of the blonde hair of one of his children or nieces or grandchildren. In contrast, my mother, who openly admitted she didn't like the look of dark-skinned people or those with obviously indigenous features (she claimed not to know why: 'because they're ugly,' she'd say, in occasional outbursts of honesty), was much more calm, friendly and unprejudiced than my father when dealing face to face with them. Tatá, who had been her nanny, and our grandmother's, was half black and half indigenous, and perhaps thanks to Tatá's very skin my mother felt genuinely fond of black and indigenous people, and was comfortable and relaxed with them.

Often what each one said didn't correspond with how they acted in real life: the agnostic acted like a mystic, and the mystic like a materialist, the idealist like an indifferent, egotistical racist, and the racist materialist like a true Christian to whom all people were equal. I suppose this was why they loved and admired each other so much: because in the passionate, generous thoughts of my father my mother saw the rationale for her life, and in her actions my father saw the practical realization of his thoughts. And sometimes the other way round: my mother saw him act like the Christian she would have liked to be in practice, and he saw her resolve daily problems like the useful and rational person he would have liked to be.

In part, my father was able to devote himself to his bursts of idealism, to his impulses of political and social assistance and work, because my mother, with her practical sense, organised the everyday life of the household. This became more and more true, as over the years, starting from her little office in the Ceiba building, and with tireless diligence and austerity, she built a medium-sized business, in charge of managing hundreds of office buildings and with thousands of employees hired and paid by her and my sisters, nearly all of whom ended up working there, by her side, like planets circling a star whose gravitational pull was too strong to resist.

My mother worked not so that she could buy more things, but so that my father could live his life without having to worry about putting food on the table. She was proud that the financial stability she provided allowed my father to speak and act without making any sort of calculation about work or monetary interests, and without having to seek work abroad, as had happened at the start of their marriage. She felt a certain amount of guilt for having made him return to the country towards the end of the fifties, when he had a secure and well-paid position in the WHO, and she had insisted they go back because she wanted to spend 'the last few short years' by my grandmother's side (who in fact lived for another three short decades, to the age of ninety-two).

For my mother there was only one place to live: Colombia. And there was only one good obstetrician, Dr. Jorge Henao Posada, because the one time she'd been attended by a different gynaecologist, in Washington, when my eldest sister was born, she had contracted puerperal fever and nearly died. Long before ultrasound scans, Dr. Henao Posada had the magical power of guessing the baby's sex before it was born, and when he put his stethoscope to the pregnant woman's belly, he would say, very gravely, 'It's going to be a boy,' or the opposite, 'It's going to be a girl.' Then he told them he was going to write it in his notebook. And later, when the baby was born, if what he'd said was right, he and the mother celebrated his powers of prescience, and if it turned out to be the opposite, he told the mother she was crazy, that he hadn't said that and he would prove it because he had it written down in his notebook, whereupon he would get the book out and show it to the woman as proof. But my mother, who had four girls in a row, discovered his trick, which was to write the opposite of what he said down in the book. Even the discovery of this trick had created a sort of complicity between the two of them, and during each of my mother's pregnancies abroad, she left my father in the sixth or seventh month and went back to Medellín, to be cared for by Dr. Henao Posada and give birth to another Colombian daughter. And when they finally came back for good, because in the end my mother's insistence bent my father's will, he ended up earning at the university the same figure which before he had earned at the WHO, three thousand, except that up there it had been dollars and here it was pesos. Perhaps for this reason my mother felt a great responsibility to work and earn some extra money so that between the two of them they would earn in Colombia what he alone had earned abroad.

It was because of the financial security she gave the family that my father was able to preserve his ideological and intellectual independence. In my parents' relationship, the ideal and the practical worked in harmony, and they were for us the image, so infrequent in this life, of a happy couple. And thanks to their example, my sisters and I understand that there is only one reason to earn decent money: to be able to preserve and defend at all costs our intellectual independence, so that no one can blackmail us into turning our backs on who we really are.

21

When my father got back from the university, he would arrive in one of two states: in a bad mood, or a good mood. If he arrived in a good mood—which was almost always as he was a generally happy person—you could hear his wonderful, resounding laughter, like the chiming of joyous bells, from the moment he came through the door. He would shout for me and my sisters, and we all came down to receive his excessive kisses, exaggerated stories, hyperbolic compliments and vast hugs. If on the other hand he got home in a bad mood, he came in without a word and furtively shut himself up in his study, put on classical music at full volume and sat down to read in his reclining chair, with the door locked. After an hour or two of this mysterious alchemy (the study was the room of transformations), this father who had come home frowning, sombre and downcast, emerged radiant and happy. Reading and listening to classical music had given him back his cheerfulness, his laughter and the desire to hug us and talk.

Without a word from my father, without being forced to read or lectured on the spiritual benefits of classical music, I understood, simply by observing the beneficial effects music and reading had on him, that one of life's great gifts is within almost everyone's reach: books and records. The downcast, bad-tempered man who would enter with his head full of the tragedies and injustices of reality, was able to regain composure and happiness through the work of great poets, thinkers and musicians.

22

I'm no longer certain exactly when, but there was a time when they left my father in peace for a few good years, and he was able to dedicate himself fully to his work. That was when he founded the National School of Public Health and became its first director, with some support from the Rockefeller Foundation (the fundamentalist left protested idiotically at this imperialist invasion, which in reality was nothing but philanthropy of the good sort, with no conditions at all aside from a simple gesture of thanks, a plaque and a letter) and from the Government. From his university chair and a few public positions (never very high, never very important and never well paid) he was able to deploy his practical knowledge throughout the whole country, and many of his undertakings during those years were a success. The indicators of health and the infant mortality rate were moving slowly but surely towards those of the most developed countries, the availability of drinking water was improving and the national mass vaccination campaigns were having the desired effect. The INCORA, the institute of agrarian reform where he worked during Lleras Restrepo's presidency, distributed a few disused estates to landless peasants. And he helped to found the Colombian Institute of Family Wellbeing, which built aqueducts and sewer systems in villages, rural districts and cities.

My father had made a sort of pragmatic alliance with a Conservative politician, another doctor, Ignacio Vélez Escobar, and this partnership, which tempered the right's distrust of my father (he couldn't be too dangerous or that much of a communist since he was with Ignacio), and the left's distrust of Vélez (he couldn't be so reactionary since he was with Héctor), achieved good things. They were both passionately devoted to saving lives, by improving basic health and hygiene conditions: clean water, a daily ration of protein, the effective disposal of excrement, and a roof to protect against the rain and the sun.

Life went on in a sort of happy routine, without any major surprises, with my mother's business steadily growing, for identical days, weeks, months and years during which we all did well at school, passed our exams with no trouble, and my father and mother got up early to go to work, without complaint, without me ever seeing or hearing, not one single day, a trace of doubt or laziness, since their work made them feel useful and successful, even 'fulfilled' (as people were beginning to say in those days). At weekends, if there were no campaigns to run in the poor neighbourhoods, we would go to Rionegro, and I'd go for long walks with my father, who recited poetry by heart as we walked, and later in the shade of a tree read *Martín Fierro*, *War and Peace*, or the poems of Barba Jacob, while my mother and sisters played cards or chatted away about boyfriends, romances and admirers, in a kind of serene harmony that seemed bound to last a lifetime.

My mother's office provided us with a standard of living we hadn't had before, and in December we all used to go to Cartagena, to the house of Uncle Rafa and Aunt Mona, my mother's sister. Uncle Rafa was an architect from the coast, a very successful, generous, hardworking man, a classmate of my aunt's at university, and they had the ideal family, as their offspring were symmetrically opposite to us: five boys and only one girl. As my father was a terrible driver, and incapable even of filling up the radiator, let alone changing a tyre, my mother went overland with my sisters in a pickup truck, choking on the dust for the twenty-eight hours the journey took, split into two exhausting days, while my father and I travelled by plane, the privileged menfolk leaving the women to run the risk and adventure of making the journey by road, while we flew in comfort in one hour to the same destination, like lords of creation. A barbarous injustice, I now realize, but back then it seemed the most natural thing in the world, since at my house everyone knew that women were the brave and practical ones, capable of anything, who faced up to life with determination and happiness, while men were spoiled, incompetent and rather useless for real life and everyday inconveniences, and only good for pontificating on truth and justice. We were ridiculous, in this and so many other ways that still haven't entirely changed, but we didn't always understand it.

They were happy years, as I was saying, but happiness is made of a flimsy substance that easily dissolves in our memories—and if we do remember it, it is often tainted with a cloying, sickly-sweet feeling that I've always rejected as harmful to living in the present: nostalgia. Of course it's also important to keep later tragedies from tarnishing happy memories, or tingeing them with misfortune, as sometimes happens when people of a certain temperament grow sick with resentment at the world after unfair or very sad things happen to them, and erase even the undeniable periods of happiness and fulfilment from their remembered past. What happened later cannot contaminate those happy years with bitterness.

So to avoid the twin dangers of nostalgia and despairing bitterness, I'll just say that in Cartagena we'd spend a whole month of happiness, and sometimes even a month and a half, or even longer, going out in Uncle Rafa's motorboat, *La Fiorella*, to Bocachica to collect seashells and eat fried fish with plantain chips and cassava, and to the Rosary Islands, where I tried lobster, or to the beach at Bocagrande, or walking to the pool at the Caribe Hotel, until we were mildly burned on our shoulders, which after a few days started peeling and turned freckly forever, or playing football with my cousins, in the little park opposite Bocagrande Church, or tennis in the Cartagena Club or ping-pong in their house, or going for bike rides, or swimming under the little nameless waterfalls along the coast, or making the most of the rain and the drowsiness of siesta time to read the complete works of Agatha Christie or the fascinating novels of Ayn Rand (I remember confusing the antics of the architect protagonist of *The Fountainhead* with those of my Uncle Rafael), or Pearl S. Buck's interminable sagas, in cool hammocks strung up in the shade on the terrace of the house, with a view of the sea, drinking Kola Román, eating Chinese empanadas on Sundays, coconut rice with red snapper on Mondays, Syrian-Lebanese kibbeh on

Wednesdays, sirloin steak on Fridays and, my favourite, egg *arepas* on Saturday mornings, piping hot and brought fresh from a nearby village, Luruaco, where they had the best recipe.

To us, the beautiful modern house my uncle had built on the bay was better designed than anything by Frank Lloyd Wright. From the terrace we could see the enormous Italian ocean liners come in (the *Verdi*, the *Rossini*, the *Donizzetti*), or the luminous ship *Gloria*, recently christened by the poet Gonzalo Arango, as she set off around the world, her white sails unfurled to the favourable Caribbean breeze, or the dark warships that slowly came and went from the naval base, their ominous cannons pointing up to the heavens. In this spacious, light-filled house, cool because it was open to the sea breeze, there was always classical music playing at full volume, echoing all around, because Uncle Rafa was (and still is) a music lover, and so all my life I have seen him surrounded by instruments or walking with the music of the spheres in his wake. He was (and still is) a violinist too, and one so resourceful that instead of his bankrupt parents paying for his studies, he had financed his architecture degree himself, by playing the violin at weddings, funerals, serenades and society balls around Medellín.

Some periods of life go by in a kind of harmonious happiness, in the tenuous key of joy, and for me they were those years, those long vacations with my cousins from the coast, who spoke a much softer, more pleasant Spanish than ours, which was harsh and mountainous, cousins whom later—when the tragedies came—we hardly ever saw again, as if we were ashamed of our sadness. Or perhaps they were sensitive enough not to wish to rub their happiness in our faces, our one-time joy having been replaced by a dark rancour, a lurking mistrust of existence and of human beings—the result of a bitterness we could not suppress and which divided us from our happy memories.

The first tragedy was about to occur through my own fault, but it didn't happen thanks to the courage of a little black boy whose name I never knew, but to whom I am eternally grateful. Because of him I did not have to spend my whole life feeling guilty for a death caused by my cowardice. We had taken the *Fiorella* out to visit a family with a holiday home on Barú Island. I could already swim, after lessons with a swimming instructor at the Hotel Caribe. El Negro Torres, a giant with a statuesque body, had spent weeks teaching the older children the crawl, breast stroke, diving, how to take in air through your mouth and expel it through your nose, the stamina required to make fins of our arms and keep our legs straight and body horizontal, until we almost drowned in exhaustion, back and forth in full-sized pools, without a break, go go go, one more length, and another, ordered El Negro Torres, an ebony sculpture in tiny white trunks, until we practically had to be pulled out by our hair, because he forced us to carry on until we sank exhausted, incapable of doing another stroke. But such agonizing training didn't do me any good, as I found out that afternoon on the island.

Bored by this long visit to Barú, after lunch, while the adults talked about politics on the porch, overheated by the topic and the weather, my youngest sister and I went to the jetty to look at the sea, and for something to do we began jumping from the jetty to the boat and the boat to the jetty. The mooring ropes grew slacker and the boat moved further and further away from the jetty, so that the jump was longer, harder to do each time, and, because of the danger, more exhilarating. I might have dared my sister, since it was very easy for me to beat her, as I was older and had longer legs.

On one of these jumps, Sol, who hadn't been to El Negro Torres's swimming lessons yet, didn't reach the boat and fell into the sea, between the jetty and the hull. I stood on the planks of the jetty looking at her, paralyzed. I watched her head sinking under the water, bubbles rising up and up from her submerged body, like an Alka-Seltzer tablet, her blonde hair emerging momentarily, and her head, a look of terror on her face, her eyes popping out and imploring, her mouth desperately taking in some air with a cough, but sinking down again immediately, and moving her little arms madly, drowning. She must have been five or six years old, and I was nine, and I knew very well that I should jump straight into the water and save her, but I was paralyzed. I just watched her, as if watching a horror film, unable to move, my body filled with the most repellent cowardice, unable to jump in and save her, unable even to shout for help, because no one would hear me anyway, what with the noise of the sea and the distance to the house, some two hundred metres from the jetty, shrouded in vegetation and palm trees.

My little sister had almost stopped coming out of the water and the motorboat was starting to move towards the jetty again, and could have hit her head, crushing her against the wooden posts, and I carried on watching, paralyzed, sure she was going to drown, trembling with fear while she died, but without moving or saying a word. Suddenly, I don't know where from, a naked black shape passed like a shadow in front of me, a dark arrow that dived into the water and came up with the little blonde girl in his arms. It was a boy the same age as me, perhaps even younger, for he was shorter than me, and he had saved her, and at that point all the adults came running from the house, shouting in alarm, in response to the uproar that had arisen from the black family's shack by the main house. I was still there, paralyzed, watching my sister cough and vomit water and cry and breathe again, in my mother's arms, until my father took me by the shoulders, squatted down to my height, looked me in the eye and said:

'Why didn't you do anything?'

He said it in a neutral, distant tone of voice, very softly. It wasn't even a reproach, rather a statement of sadness, of confused disappointment: why didn't you do anything, why didn't you do anything. And I still don't know why I didn't do anything, or rather I do, because I'm a coward, because I was scared that if I jumped in to save her I would drown too, but it was an unjustifiable fear, as the little black boy showed me how all it took was one second, one act of bravery and one determined gesture so that life could go on and not turn into the most horrific tragedy. And although my sister didn't drown, I was left forever with the horrible feeling, the deep-seated suspicion that maybe, if I ever find myself in a position where I have to demonstrate what I'm made of, I will be a coward.

23

Perhaps it was with the aim of strengthening my character a little that, shortly after this episode, maybe a year or two later, my father decided the moment had come for me to see a dead person. The occasion arose early one morning when he was called to the morgue in Medellín to identify John Gómez, a mentally disabled boy who'd been hit by a car on the motorway, the only son of Octavia, one of my father's aunts. Before he left to carry out the task, my father woke me up and said:

'We're going to the lecture theatre, I think it's time you saw a dead person.'

I got dressed very happily, as if going on a fun day out, since I'd been asking him to introduce me to the world of what no longer exists for a long time. We left the house together, and from the moment we entered El Pedregal morgue, next to the Universal Cemetery, I didn't like it. The hall was full of corpses, but I didn't want to look at any of them, never mind that most of them were covered in sheets. It smelled of blood and butchery and formaldehyde and decay. My father led me by the hand to where the pathologist showed him the body of the boy that might be John. And it was John, so the doctor suggested my father attend the autopsy. My memories from then on are not very clear. I see a hand saw starting to cut open the cranium, I see blue intestines being deposited into a bucket, I see a broken tibia poking through the calf, breaking the skin. I smell a strong smell of blood mixed with that of formaldehyde, like a cross between an abattoir and a chemistry laboratory. Afterwards, when my father understood how shocked I had been by the spectacle of the autopsy, he decided to take me for a walk among the other dead bodies. The previous evening a light aircraft had crashed on the outskirts of Medellín, and there were several charred, destroyed bodies I couldn't look at closely without retching. But perhaps what I remember most clearly is the body of a teenage girl, completely naked, transparent and pale, with a blue knife wound to her abdomen. A label attached to her big toe said she had been stabbed in a bar in Guayaquil, and my father said, 'Maybe she was a prostitute, poor thing.' It was the first time I'd seen a naked woman (other than my sisters); the first time I had seen a prostitute; the first time I really *saw* a dead person. At that point I fainted. I next see myself outside the morgue, being made to drink a sickeningly sweet grape soda, to revive me, pale, speechless, and sweating.

For several nights I couldn't sleep. I had nightmares in which I saw John's broken bones, torn flesh and blue intestines by my bed, the same dark blue as the stab wound on the girl from Guayaquil, and her whole body appeared once more in my mind, in all its paleness, with her downy pubis, coagulated blood on her side. (Years later, a sick fascination I couldn't fathom at the time made me want to buy a shocking painting called 'Girl Showing Her Wound,' in which a young girl points out the buttonhole of a stab wound on her abdomen. Now that I recall this visit to El Pedregal morgue, I think I understand why I bought this painting, which everyone who visits me finds disturbing.) Over the bad nights that followed, my father felt guilty and remorseful. He sat on the floor by my bed and stayed with me for hours, explaining things to me as he stroked my head or read me peaceful stories. And each time he saw in my eyes that the horrific images had come back, he asked for my forgiveness. Maybe he had thought that my life was too easy, too nice, and he wanted to show me the most painful, tragic and absurd sides of existence, as a lesson. If he'd been able to see into the future, perhaps he would have decided that this early form of shock therapy was completely unnecessary.

24

We remember our childhood not as a smooth timeline but a series of shocks. Memory is an opaque, cracked mirror; or, rather, memories are like timeless seashells scattered over a beach of oblivion. I know that lots of things happened in those years, but trying to remember them is as futile as trying to remember a dream, a dream that leaves behind it a feeling without images, like a scene without a story, an emptiness, just a vague mood. The years, the words, the games, the caresses have faded, but nevertheless, suddenly, as one goes back over the past, something lights up again in a dark forgotten region. For me it's nearly always a sensation of embarrassment mixed with happiness, and my father's face is nearly always there, right up close to mine like the shadow that follows us, or that we ourselves follow.

Shortly before or after my younger sister almost drowned, I learned another lesson from her, without her meaning to teach me, and this lesson coincided with another disappointment for my father. My father took

Sol and me, the two youngest children, to a Public Book Fair in the centre of Medellín. When we got there he said we could each choose one book, whichever we wanted, and he would buy it for us, to read and enjoy later at home. First we would look at all the stalls in the fair, and then, on the way back, we could choose the book that we most wanted.

We walked around the fair twice, up and down the street, and my father, without pushing us too much, gave us some suggestions, picking up books and praising the story, the talent of the writer, the thrilling plot. My sister soon chose one on his recommendation: *The Happy Prince and Other Tales* by Oscar Wilde, in a very modest but pretty edition, white, with a red rose on the cover. In the meantime, on my tour of the fair I had become obsessed with a big, expensive book with a red jacket, called *The Official Rules of All the World's Sports*. Now, if there was anything my father despised it was sport, and exercise in general, which to him was merely a possible source of injuries and accidents. He tried to dissuade me. He said it wasn't literature, or science, or history. He even said, unusually for him, that it was very expensive. But I was set on the book and, gritting his teeth in annoyance, my father bought it for me.

When we got home later, the three of us went into his study, and while I attempted to learn the rules of American football, which neither then nor ever after have I been able to comprehend, my father began reading one of the Oscar Wilde stories, *The Nightingale and the Rose*, to my sister. They must have been a page into the story when, already totally bored by the incomprehensible rules of American football (which neither then nor ever after have I been able to understand), I began secretly to listen to Wilde's wonderful story. At the end, when the bird dies, pierced by the thorn of the rose, I shut my book and went over to them, humbled and repentant. My father was brimming with emotion as he finished the reading, and I felt as miserable as the time I was unable to save my sister when she fell into the sea—and my father was, I believe, as disappointed in me as he had been then. Afterwards I hid the big red book of sports rules behind my other books, as if it were a pornographic magazine, and read Wilde's fascinating stories over and over again. And since then I have read nothing but literature, science, and history, and as a result have never learned the rules of cricket, rugby, American football or judo.

25

'Sorry, I didn't know you were busy,' my father said.

It was a hot summer's evening, and he had come home with a gift for me, a biography of Goethe, which he later gave to me (I still have it and still haven't read it: there'll be time for it), but when he came into my room, I was engaged in that manual exercise that for all adolescent boys is an exquisite and urgent pressure. He usually knocked before entering my bedroom, but on this particular evening he didn't; happy in anticipation of giving me the book, he simply opened the door. I had a hammock hanging up in my room, and there I lay, in full swing, looking at a magazine to help my hand and imagination along. He paused for a moment, smiled, and turned to leave. And before he closed the door, he said those words: 'Sorry, I didn't know you were busy.'

He said nothing further on the subject until weeks later, in his study, he told me a story: 'When I was in the last year of Med School, one of my cousins, Luis Guillermo Echeverri Abad, asked me over to his house. After all manner of mysterious hesitations and false starts, this cousin confessed that he was very concerned about his son, Fabito, who apparently thought of nothing but wanking. Morning, noon and night. You're almost a doctor, my cousin said to me, talk to him, give him some advice, tell him how dangerous the solitary vice is. And so,' my father continued, 'I went and spoke to my cousin's son and I said to him: "Relax, keep on doing it as much as you want. It's not bad for you and it's totally normal—it would be strange for a young boy not to masturbate. But I'll give you some advice: don't let your father catch you and don't leave any evidence." Shortly after this my cousin called again, to thank me. I'd performed a miracle: Fabito, as if by magic, had given up the vice.' And my father, as if the whole story were just one big joke, burst out laughing.

I was always aware of my father's confidence in me. He accepted whatever I did, and though he had high hopes for me, always assured me that I didn't need to achieve anything in life, that my mere existence, whatever form it took and as long as I was happy, was enough to make him happy. His faith in me was a burden of sorts (I might betray his hopes or prove his confidence unfounded), but it was an agreeable one, and not excessive, because anything I did, no matter how trivial and ridiculous, pleased him. He was excited by the first scribbles I made on a page, and later he interpreted my crazy changes of direction as excellent formative experiences, forgave my inconstancy as a genetic trait from which he too suffered, and regarded my general instability in life and ideology as inevitable in a world that was transforming before our eyes, and for which a person needed a flexible mind to know which side to take.

Never—neither when I changed degree courses four

times in quick succession, nor when I was expelled from university for writing an article against the Pope; neither when I was unemployed with a daughter to look after, nor when I moved in with my girlfriend without getting married—did I ever hear a word of criticism or complaint from him, only the most tolerant and open acceptance of my life and independence. And I think he was like that with all my sisters as well: never one to condemn, never a critic or an inquisitor, much less a castigator or jailer, always a liberal, open, positive person, who accepted our mistakes as if they were innocent pranks. Maybe he believed that all human beings are condemned to be what they are, and there is no stick that will straighten us out, or bad company that will corrupt us. Perhaps he was lucky too, since none of us turned out dissolute, sickly, lazy, idiotic or useless. If we had, I don't know how he would have reacted, but I imagine it would have been with the same open, tolerant, happy attitude, though mingled inevitably with pain and impotence.

In matters of sex he was always very open, as the masturbation episode shows (and there are other examples I won't mention because there's nothing more embarrassing than the sex lives of one's own parents; we always imagine our parents as asexual beings—as a friend of mine says, 'mothers don't even pee.'). It's true that my father was more of a puritan in real life than in theory, and in spite of himself something of a traditionalist in family matters, though theoretically very liberal. Here, too, he was the opposite of my mother, who in theory claimed to follow the teachings of the Holy Mother Church, but in practice was more open and liberal than my father. Once when the husband of one of my cousins, a member of Opus Dei, gave a lecture at the university criticizing the use of condoms and maintaining that sometimes medicine was the perverse ally of human immorality, making it possible for people to do with impunity what was forbidden by God, my mother secretly told this cousin of mine that, though she agreed with her husband, she nevertheless recommended that every time he went on a trip she should put a box of condoms in his suitcase, because men were very good at making speeches about morals, but at the moment of truth, at the point of temptation, morals were the last things on their minds, and in that case, it would be better at least that he, and above all she, didn't end up getting ill due to an excess of abstract morality, instead of staying healthy thanks to a bit of practical immorality. I could talk to my father about all these intimate matters, and ask him about them directly, as he was never shocked, and would listen calmly, replying in a tone somewhere between devoted and didactic, never judgemental. Halfway through adolescence, at the all-boys school I attended, something happened that tormented me for years. The sight of my classmates' genitals, and their erotic games, excited me, and I came to the anguished conclusion that I must be gay. I told this to my father racked with fear and shame, and he replied, smiling calmly, that it was too soon to know for certain, that I should wait until I had more life experience, that during adolescence we were so full of hormones that anything could be a turn-on, a chicken, a donkey, a pair of mating salamanders or dogs, but this didn't mean I was homosexual. And above all, he tried to make it clear that if I were, it wouldn't matter either, as long as I chose whatever made me happy, what my deepest inclinations suggested, because one shouldn't go against the nature one had been born with, whatever it might be, and being homosexual or heterosexual was the same as being right- or left-handed, except that left-handed people were slightly less common than right-handed ones. The only slight problem I might have if I defined myself as homosexual, would be a bit of social discrimination, in a country as obtuse as ours, but this too was manageable with equal doses of indifference and pride, discretion and outrage, and above all with a sense of humour, because the worst thing would be not to be what one is. On this last point he laid an emphasis that showed that it rose from a very deep part of his conscience, letting me know that the most serious, the most harmful thing one could do to oneself, was to pretend to be what one is not, or to hide what one is—symmetrical evils, and both sure-fire recipes for unhappiness as well as for bad taste. In any case, he said, with a wisdom and generosity I'm still thankful for, and with a calm that still calms me, I should wait a while until I had spent more time with women, to see if I didn't feel the same way about them, or even more so.

And that's what happened, after some time, and also after talking—paid for, although not prompted by, my father—to a psychiatrist and a psychoanalyst about my worries (Ricardo José Toro and Claudia Nieva, both fondly remembered). As I talked to them, or perhaps I should say as I poured into their ears the anxieties of my still maturing brain, I managed to discover for myself the course of my most profound desires, which thanks to luck or my own dullness have ended up coinciding with the well-trodden path of the majority. However, since that time I've never been afraid of my darkest desires, and don't feel guilty or anguished by them. If I have occasionally been attracted to forbidden things, like another man's wife, for example, or women much younger than me, or my friends' girlfriends, I haven't tormented myself over these infringements, but instead viewed them as the body's stubborn, yet blind and essentially innocent demands, which must be reined in or not, according to the damage they might do to others and to oneself—indeed with this sole criterion, more pragmatic and direct than that of an absolute, abstract morality, of religious dogma that doesn't change with circumstances, time or opportunity, but which is always the same, with an inflexibility harmful to society and to individuals.

26

After this interlude of near-perfect happiness, which lasted for years, heaven remembered our family and became jealous, and the furious God my ancestors believed in unleashed his wrath upon us. We were a happy family, though perhaps we didn't realize it; very happy, in fact. It nearly always happens this way: when we are touched by happiness we hardly realize we're happy, and then maybe we're sent a good dose of pain from on high, so that we learn to be grateful. This is one of my mother's explanations, which explains nothing, and which I'm not endorsing or putting forward as my own, but am writing because it is true that, while we feel we deserve happiness and it seems natural to us, tragedies seem sent from elsewhere, decreed by evil forces for dark sins, or by avenging gods, or angels executing inescapable sentences.

Yes. We were happy because my father had returned from Asia for good and wasn't planning ever to go away again, since on his last trip he had grown depressed to the very point of suicide. Moreover, he was no longer being persecuted in the university for being a communist; indeed, if anything, he was considered reactionary (because he seemed to be happy, and to a Communist, anyone happy amid so many unhappy, deprived people must be reactionary). We were happy because for a time it seemed that those in power in Medellín trusted my father and let him get on with his work, as they could see he was carrying out useful public health programmes: vaccinations, training health promoters, building rural aqueducts, and was able to convert his words into action, unlike so many others. When my father saw that his work was no longer in danger and my mother started to earn more money than he did, we began to allow ourselves certain luxuries, such as occasionally going to a Chinese restaurant together, or opening a bottle of wine, an unusual, almost unique occasion, when Dr. Saunders was there. There were better Christmas presents too (a bicycle, a cassette recorder), and I remember going as a family to see a film my father thought was the best he'd ever seen: *Born Free* (I remember the title, the queue to get into the Lido Cinema, but nothing else about it).

We were happy because no one in the family had died and every weekend we went to the farm, a small farm, the size of two city blocks, in Llanogrande, up in the mountains, which Uncle Luis, the sickly priest, had left to my mother along with his life savings. My father even bought me a horse, Amigo, a skinny black hack with a white forehead, all gangly, with the same look about him as Rocinante, and skinnier by the week, with ever more prominent ribs because there was no grass on the farm, but to me he seemed like an Arabian colt or perhaps an Andalusian thoroughbred, when I went galloping along the roads around the farm, and since then I have associated happiness with the streets of Cartagena, or with riding horseback through the countryside, with no one talking to me, not having to talk to anyone, just me and my horse, like the Lone Ranger, which was my favourite comic book, its protagonist a sort of Quixote *sans* Sancho who rights wrongs on the plains of Texas or Tijuana or somewhere I recognized was not part of this world, but of the world beyond that comic books represent.

The day the horse arrived on the farm, however, I received, or, rather, failed to receive a message from life, and which, had I possessed the wisdom experience should (but almost never does) give us, would have warned me of how happiness is threatened by misfortune at every moment. My father had bought him as a surprise, and that Saturday at noon, when we got to Llanogrande he stopped the car on the cattle grid and pointed towards the field: 'Look, there's what you wanted, a horse.' My heart leapt for joy. At last I could have what I liked most of all about Grandfather's farm (riding) without having to undergo the pain of being separated from my father overnight. So I leapt out of the car, our old sky-blue Plymouth, hurriedly opening the door, jumped to the ground, and slammed the door shut with all my strength so I could run to the horse. But I was in such a rush that I caught two fingers in the car door and crushed them. I felt a piercing pain. Happiness and pleasure turned into an awful nightmare. One of my nails came off and both fingers went purple with blood. My happy laughter was mixed with tears, and I only got to meet Amigo some time later, my fingers in a bowl of ice to soothe the pain and swelling. I was laughing and crying at the same time. Maybe this experience of happiness suddenly tinged with pain should have taught me that our happiness is always precariously balanced, unstable, on the verge of sliding down a precipice of grief.

But it didn't. Back then we thought life would always be good, and had no reason to doubt it. We were happy because my sisters were all pretty and cheerful, the prettiest girls in the neighbourhood of Laureles, everyone said so, Maryluz, Clara, Vicky (we called Eva Vicky, because she's called Eva Victoria, but hated the name Eva, she thought it sounded like a backwoods mountain name, and this always bothered her, though I think it's the only pretty name in the family) and Marta. Sol did not take part in their shenanigans yet because she was still very young, and only watched her sisters, hidden next to me at the window, telling tales of furtive kisses, as did I ('Mummy, Jorge kissed Clara and Clara let him'; 'Mummy, Álvaro tried to kiss Vicky but Vicky didn't let him'; 'Mummy, Marta kissed Hernán Darío and he put his hand on her booby'). But soon her time would come for secret kisses and fun too. Yes, my sisters were the prettiest girls in Laureles, anyone who knew them will tell you it's true; the nicest, most cheerful, flirtatious, wittiest girls, and the house swarmed with college and university students, madly buzzing about at all hours to win their hearts, because they smiled and laughed and loved to dance. All the boys in Laureles were crazy about them, and came from as far away as the centre of town and El Poblado to see them, even during the day, to pay them a visit quaking with shyness, drunk with the fear of rejection. And at night too, on Fridays and Saturdays after midnight, the daytime visitors began to reappear, desperately in love, and endless serenades took place in front of our house. Mary was serenaded by her boyfriend

Fernando, to whom she was faithful from the age of eleven, never letting anyone else come near her, and if another boy did come to serenade her she would stop him in his tracks and shout at him to go away. Clara had her two boyfriends and twenty admirers (once she was serenaded four times in a single night, in four different styles, the last one accompanied by mariachis, in a contest to see who would go furthest to win her heart of steel), because although she wasn't fickle she was so pretty that she found it impossible to choose between so many perfect catches, each one better than the last. One of them, Santamaría, even committed suicide out of lovesickness. Vicky was serenaded by a certain Álvaro Uribe, a very short boy, who was crazy about her, but she wasn't quite so keen, as she thought he was too serious, bad-tempered and rude. 'Since you ignore me,' he said once, 'I'm going to exchange you.' And he named his best mare Vicky, because he liked horses more than anything else, and started to say, 'Now I ride Vicky every week.' He brought his grades for her to see: top marks in everything. But in the penultimate year of college he was expelled, because of another of my sisters, not Vicky, but Maryluz, who was older. The college queen was being chosen at the Benedictine charity ball, and Maryluz was the queen of the sixth year; the queen of the fifth year, Álvaro's year, was another girl, and right up till the last minute she was winning. It wasn't the prettiest girl who won, but the one who collected the most money, and the fifth year girl had collected more, because Álvaro's father, a rancher, was rich, and had donated a lot. The die was cast, but at the last moment Maryluz asked one of the richest men in Medellín, Alfonso Mora de la Hoz, for a donation, and he gave her a big fat cheque. When the money was counted, the fifth year queen was in the lead, and Álvaro was pleased, but the last piece of paper they took out was the cheque from the super-rich man, so Maryluz ended up with the most. There were shouts of congratulation for her from the crowd, but then Álvaro, who always was a bad loser, got up on a desk and harangued the students, in a revolutionary tone: 'The Benedictine monks have sooooooold out!' And the Benedictine monks expelled him, for being unable to accept defeat and the rules of the game, and he had to finish his secondary education at Jorge Robledo College, where all the expelled school-kids went. Then Vicky went out with another Uribe, Federico, who wasn't related to the first one, but from a different Uribe family, and she ended up marrying him. When it came to choosing between them, my father said, 'This one's better; the other's too ambitious. I don't know if he'd be faithful.' Neither was faithful, but that's by the by. And Marta, because she was younger, from another generation, wasn't serenaded with trios, which was old-fashioned, something adults and old people did, but instead sometimes a car would pull up, its door would open, and suddenly the speakers would erupt with the sound of drums and electric guitars, with songs by the Beatles or the Rolling Stones, and later the Carpenters, Cat Stevens, David Bowie or Elton John. There was already a generation gap between my four elder sisters, with Marta being the first one who belonged to my generation, although really I don't think I belong to one at all, for when she died, I was left bereft of influence. Maybe this is why I devoted myself to classical music, which was firm ground, my father's, and maybe also why I have never serenaded anyone, or risked trios, *bambuco* folk music or mariachis, nor even rock music from car speakers.

And now I must tell the story of Marta's death, because this was the watershed, the event that splits my family's story in two.

27

Marta Cecilia to my mother, Taché to my father, Marta to her siblings, she was the star of the family. Ever since she was a little girl it was clear that none of us was as cheerful, as intelligent or as full of life (and believe me there was competition, and very tough competition, from my other sisters). At the age of five, she began to play the violin, and from time to time went to the conservatoire, where a Czech teacher—Joseph Matza, an extraordinary musician who had been first violinist with the Freiburg Opera—said it had been years since he had seen as much talent as he saw in Marta. Somewhat out of his milieu in these tropics, Matza conducted the University Band on weekends (sometimes on a Sunday my father would take us to hear a concert in Bolívar Park) and got our sad little orchestra to play everything he could. He ended up an embittered alcoholic, and his students would pick him up off the street in the early hours of the morning, but even the beggars looked out for him, saying: 'The maestro's drunk, let him sleep.' In his lessons, Maestro Matza would tell his pupils, looking at his instrument with devoted rage, 'This is my closest enemy.' Maybe that explains why, by the age of eleven, my sister Marta had grown bored of the violin, deciding it was a very sad instrument, demanding unwavering devotion and made for playing old music, whereas she was very modern, from the rock era. So she gave up the violin with no regrets and without upsetting my mother and father, who never put any pressure on us, and started playing guitar and singing. She exchanged Maestro Matza and his 'close enemy' for the friendlier guitar and a Colombian teacher, Sonia Martínez, who taught *bambuco* folk songs that Marta wasn't terribly keen on, but at the same time excellent vocal technique and guitar accompaniment. She learned more with Andrés Posada, her first boyfriend, who is now an extraordinary musician, and Pilar, Andrés' sister, another great musician, and the three of them would spend the afternoons together singing songs by the Beatles, Joan Manuel Serrat, Cat Stevens, and I don't know who else.

By the age of fourteen she was already singing in a group, the Cuarteto Ellas, with another extraordinary singer, Claudia Gómez, and Marta was the first person in our family to win prizes for performing (in truth she was the only one) and appeared in the newspapers and on some television programmes. She used to go on tour all over Colombia, and they went to Puerto Rico, San Andrés and Miami, places her siblings couldn't even dream of seeing. Marta was also a natural actress and would recite lengthy speeches by heart at my older sisters' parties when they turned fifteen, which was the most important age for a young woman in those days: the age she was 'presented to society.' And she was also the best student in her class at La Enseñanza School, and adored by her classmates, because she wasn't an irritating nerd, but a cheerful student who could learn a lesson after hearing it only once, and didn't have to study. She read more than I did, and was so quick and brilliant that my father liked her best of all of us, even more than me, who had the dubious distinction of being the only boy, and more than my eldest sister, who because she was the eldest and so good to him was always the apple of his eye.

My two eldest sisters got married. Maryluz to her eternal boyfriend, Fernando Vélez, an economist who was wealthy by the age of twenty thanks to a large inheritance from his father, the founder of Líster Laboratories, a pharmaceutical company, who died prematurely of cancer. But the economist was very generous, and no good at economizing, and even worse in league with my sister, who was very open-handed, just like my father; for her there was no greater pleasure than doing favours for others and giving away everything she had, her belongings, her time, her money, her clothes, everything. The two of them, Maryluz and Fernando, were as one, a pair of Siamese twins, and it seemed as if they had been married ever since their first communion. He was thirteen when he serenaded my sister, then eleven, for the first time. When she turned seventeen, they had been together for so long they could no longer bear all that virginity (those were the days of no sex before marriage), so she called him to order and made him marry her before he'd even finished university. Then Clara felt pressured to get married soon as well so as not to be left behind, and three years later she married 'the kid with the best future in Medellín,' Jorge Humberto Botero, a lawyer, 'divinely handsome' according to all the girls, extremely nice and very intelligent, my father said, even though he spoke in a rather flowery manner (which made us all laugh a little, partly in admiration), using a slow, didactic, intellectual tone of voice. As far as I know he is the only person in the world who still uses the future subjunctive ('if such a thing should chance to happen'), and he was among the first Colombians to go to jogging in the streets, like the gringos do. He was trim and good-looking and his artificial way of speaking was so constant that one could almost say artifice was his natural way of being. After they got married, Clara and Jorge Humberto moved to the United States, to continue their studies at the University of West Virginia in the city of Morgantown.

By then there were only four children left at home. Eva Victoria, now the oldest, had become a very elegant young lady. She spent the whole day with one of her classmates, María Emma Mejía, who advised her on her wardrobe and how to be glamorous, and taught her how to move her hands like a ballerina. It is perhaps thanks to María Emma's lessons that Eva, or Vicky, has the best manners in our family, as if she came from a better class of people than the rest of us, and a haughty demeanour born not of disdain, but rather, it seems to me, of restraint. In my opinion, she examines her conscience unduly, living in fear of the obscure, uncertain guilt that is known as original sin: she suffers from her rectitude, which sometimes almost stops her from living, making her see wickedness and a lack of decency everywhere, even where there is no sign of them.

After Eva Victoria came Marta and then me. Marta, the star, the singer, the best student, the actress. She was very observant, and had an extremely good ear and a talent for perfect imitation. Within a minute of meeting someone she could mimic their gestures and their voice, the way they walked or cut their food up, the tics in their eyes or hands and mispronunciations. Pity whoever came to our house: as soon as they left, my sister would perform not a simple impression, but more of an x-ray examination of their deepest being. Marta intimidated me; in a way she made me feel not only younger, which I was, but smaller in every sense. She always had the exact phrase, a brilliant crack, an appropriate remark for everything, while I was still struggling to untangle a knot of words that wouldn't even bubble up from my mind let alone reach the tip of my tongue. But deep down this inferiority didn't bother me too much, as I had yielded to her superiority from the outset, and taken refuge in books, in the serene rhythm of books, in the slow, serious conversations with my father, which cleared up my physical and metaphysical doubts, and the fact that my sister was superior was something it was impossible to doubt or compete against, like comparing Medellín's diminutive Pandeazúcar Hill with the Nevado del Ruiz volcano. Maybe because I couldn't compete with her at speaking or dancing or singing or acting or mimicking or studying, I became a reader and a lone ranger, an average student with little talent for oral expression, rather inept at sports, and always good at only one thing: writing.

The youngest was Sol, who still hadn't emerged from the mists of infancy, and spent all day at Mónica and Claudia's house, cousins the same age as her and who lived on the same block, playing mummies and babies with a seriousness real mothers can only aspire to, with pretend Barbie daughters and little toy cars and multiple outfits and costumes and plastic dolls. Solbia (we called her Solbia because her full name is Sol Beatriz) was really more our aunt and uncle's daughter than my father and mother's, and sometimes, in arguments, although she is the only doctor in the family now, and a studious, professional woman, comes out with manners more suited to a farmer than a physician, which she can only have inherited from Uncle Antonio, a rancher, and the one of my grandfather's sons who most resembled him.

And that was when God, or rather absurd fate, began to envy so much happiness, and smote this happy family with merciless fury. One evening, arriving home from work, my father called Sol and me. He looked serious, more serious than ever; not in a bad mood, however, but with a deeply worried expression, as if he had a terrible problem, his hands twitching, his mouth tense, overcome by nerves. Something very strange must be happening, as this was totally out of the ordinary; his arrival was usually a flood of happiness, laughter and jokes, or else the ritual of sombre music and restorative reading. Not this time: come with me for a drive in the car, he said, his voice brusque and stern. He started the car and after driving round and round the labyrinthine streets of Laureles, he pulled up in an empty side street, near La América, on the corner of San Juan. He stopped the car and then began slowly, turning to look us in the eye:

'I have something very difficult and very important to tell you.' His voice was pained and my father paused to swallow. 'You must be very strong and take it calmly. Look, it's hard to say. Marta is very ill. She has a disease called melanoma. It's a kind of cancer, a skin cancer.'

I, instead of controlling myself, sprang up and said the worst possible thing, which was the first thought that occurred to me:

'So she's going to die.'

My father, who did not want to hear this, much less think it, because it was what he most feared and what he knew, in the depths of his soul, would inevitably happen, got angry with me:

'I didn't say that, damn it! We're going to take her to the United States and she might get better. We're going to do everything humanly possible to save her. You two have to be strong, and calm, and you have to help. She doesn't know what's wrong with her, and you have to treat her really well, and not say anything, at least for now, while we prepare her. Medicine has made huge advances and, if there is any possibility, we are going to cure her.'

Then four months of searing pain began, from August to December, from which none of us emerged unscathed.

Cancer, at the age of sixteen, and in a girl like Marta, causes unbearable pain and denial. There is a point when a human life is at its most valuable, and this moment, I believe, coincides with the peak that comes at the end of adolescence. Parents spend many years looking after and modelling the person who will represent and replace them; eventually this person starts flying solo, and in this case, she flies very well, much better than her parents and everyone else they know. The death of a newborn baby, or an old person, hurts less. There is a sort of increasing curve in the value of human life, and the peak, I believe, is between fifteen and thirty years old; after this the curve begins, slowly, once more, to descend, until at a hundred years it again coincides with that of a foetus, and hardly matters to us at all.

28

In Washington there was a hospital that was running trials of the newest treatments for this sinister cancer, melanoma. My father and mother sold things; my father's car and the first office my mother had bought, in the La Ceiba building, with her years of savings, so they could afford the treatment. Several friends, Jorge Fernández and Marta Hernández, Fabio Ortega and Mabel Escobar, Don Emilio Pérez, and my brother-in-law Fernando Vélez, gave them thousands of dollars in cash, as a loan, with no repayment date, or as a gift, and my father and mother took this money with tears in their eyes. When they returned from the States, my father and mother gave back the loans unspent, but just having the money in their wallets made them feel safe. They were prepared to sell the house, the farm, everything we owned, if there was a cure for Marta, because that's how healthcare was up there, and still is—better for those who could afford the most money to pay for it. As it turned out, no amount of money could cure this cancer, but at the time there were vague hopes for a new drug, in the first stages of experimentation, and they started to give it to her in the hospital.

In Washington they stayed with Édgar Gutiérrez Castro, who gave them his whole apartment and went to stay in a room at a friend's house. When he was on his way to pick them up from the airport, he was so anxious that he crashed, and by the time he turned up in a taxi my father, mother and Marta were gone. They had taken a bus to a hotel, thinking Édgar had forgotten to pick them up. He collected them from the hotel and installed them in his apartment, 'for as long as necessary,' an act of generosity my family will never forget. My sister Clara came over from West Virginia to stay with them, and Jorge Humberto, her husband, also came at the weekends. There, on Édgar Gutiérrez's balcony, Marta at last asked my father the fateful question: 'Daddy, is it true I've got cancer?' And he, his eyes flooded with tears in despair, could only nod his head, but he also added a white lie that sounded true: it was cancer, yes, but as it was skin cancer it was very superficial, and very treatable. He didn't think she was going to die. My father wanted her spirit to aid an improbable recovery. And she never asked him again. From that day on she managed to control her pain and keep her spirits up with a distant hope. The fact is she tried to be happy until the end.

One weekend they took her on a trip, with the hospital's authorization, to see New York City. They went with Clara and were walking through Manhattan when Marta felt terribly dizzy and fainted, her heart beating abnormally fast. They had to call an ambulance and rush back to Washington in it. This single ambulance journey cost them the same amount they'd received for selling my father's car. It wasn't serious, just a reaction to a very strong drug she'd been given, maybe an early form of chemotherapy.

When they finally discovered that Marta's cancer had metastasized, my parents were told that the only thing to be done was to wait and see what effects the new drug might have. They could take the doses back to Colombia and send the lab results to the hospital each week, where the specialists would analyze them, and if necessary, they would give them further instructions over the phone. When Clara took them to the airport, the day they went home, she said goodbye to Marta with a long kiss and a big hug. Marta told her she was scared, and Clara laughed at her, said don't be so silly, everything's going to be fine. And she said it with a false happy smile. When she got back to the car park, after leaving them at immigration, Clara felt something running down her legs, a warm liquid. She ran to the bathroom. She had an uncontrollable haemorrhage, rivers of blood that ran down from her vagina onto the floor and she had to go to hospital (a different one, in the city where she lived) so they could staunch the flow of blood by performing a curettage on her, and they even had to put her on a drip and give her transfusions. Perhaps, said the doctors, she'd been pregnant without realizing and had a miscarriage. It could be explained, they told her, by the great emotional pain she was in.

When they got back from the States, Marta began to slip away day by day, very slowly, bit by bit, so that we could clearly see how death was taking over, centimetre by centimetre, the body of this pretty sixteen-year-old girl, who a year earlier had been the very picture of health, vitality and joy, the very image of happiness. Every day she grew paler and thinner, becoming nothing but skin and bones, weaker and in more pain every day, and more fragile, until she almost disappeared. In the same way that the essence can be extracted from a flower to make perfume, or the spirit distilled from wine, at times the suffering and pain in our lives is concentrated and distilled until it becomes devastating, unbearable. This is how it was with my sister Marta's death, which destroyed my family, maybe forever.

They had found the cancer on her neck, at the base of her skull, at the back, a line of little lumps, or rather a rosary, that's what they said, a rosary of little lumps with a softish consistency, one after the other, a rosary, yes, like the ones Uncle Luis and Grandma Victoria brandished, yes, a metastasized rosary, this was what God and the Most Holy Virgin had sent us, after the Dawn Rosary, after the innumerable rosaries in my grandma's house, a cancer rosary, that's right, a succession of fatal pearls set just under the surface of the skin. This is what this happy, innocent girl deserved for the sins committed by my father or me or my mother, or by her or our grandparents and great-grandparents or who knows who.

Marta was in the best hands, in the care of the leading lights of medicine, first in Washington, and later in Medellín, with my father's friends and colleagues from the Faculty of Medicine. There was Dr. Borrero, a wise man, the best internist in the city, and a fount of scientific knowledge who had saved thousands of old people, children and youngsters from every kind of ailment, the most serious diseases, lung cancer, heart and kidney failure, but who couldn't do anything for Marta. Dr. Borrero came to the house every evening, and he didn't just help Marta, alleviating her pain, but above all he helped my father and mother, so they didn't go mad with grief. Alberto Echavarría, the haematologist who had saved children from ferocious forms of leukaemia, and treated sickle-cell anaemia, and cured haemophiliacs, also came, but he couldn't do anything for Marta, only give her a blood test every two or three days, so he could put together charts of blood work to be sent periodically to the United States, so they could see what effect the drug was having and how the disease was slowly progressing towards death. Eduardo Abad was there, a great heart and lung specialist and my father's uncle, who cured people with tuberculosis and pneumonia, but who could only confirm that the cancer had also spread to Marta's lungs. And Dr. Escorcia, the most distinguished cardiologist around, who had brought people back to life after heart attacks, who had performed open heart surgery, who was getting ready for the first transplants, but couldn't do anything for Marta's heart, which grew worse week after week, and she began to suffer from cardiac arrhythmia, an abnormally fast heart beat, and sudden spasms, and all kinds of other things, maybe because the cancer had metastasized to her heart, liver, throat, and, worst of all, her brain.

Sometimes, my father shut himself up in his study and put one of Beethoven's symphonies on at full volume, or a piece by Mahler (his painful *Kindertotenlieder*), and beneath the chords of the orchestra playing *tutti*, I could hear his sobs, his cries of despair as, behind the locked door, he cursed heaven, he cursed himself, for being stupid, for being useless, for not having removed all my sister's moles in time, for letting her sunbathe in Cartagena, for not having studied more, for anything, venting all his impotence and pain, unable to bear what he was seeing, his darling little girl who was slipping out of his doctor's hands, unable to do a thing to prevent it, just trying with a thousand morphine injections to alleviate her awareness of death at least, of the final decline of her body, and of the pain. I would sit on the floor outside the study door, like a little dog whose owner won't let him in, and listen to the cries that seeped out from the gap under the door, which came from inside him, from deep down, as if from the centre of the earth, with an uncontrollable pain, and then at last they would stop, and the music would play on for a while, and he would come out again, his eyes red and a false smile on his lips, hiding the boundless extent of his pain, and see me there, 'what are you doing down there, my love,' and make me stand up, and hug me, before going up to Marta's room with a happy expression, to cheer her up. I went in after him, to tell her that surely tomorrow she'd start to feel better, when the drug started to take effect, when the cure started working, that foul pap, that whitish brew with an iridescent sparkle to it they had brought from the United States and that she had to swallow down in disgust, by the spoonful, a drug still being tested and which made her worse, much worse, and in the end didn't do a thing, didn't even bring us hope, and which they decided one day she should stop taking, because week after week the tests that Echa, the haematologist, did came out worse, and worse, and worse.

Occasionally, Marta livened up a little. She was pale, almost transparent, and each day she weighed less. You could see the fragility in her every finger, in every bone of her body, in her blonde hair that was falling out in handfuls. But some sunny mornings she would go out to the patio, walking very slowly, almost like an old woman, and ask for her guitar, and sing a very sweet song, with a happy theme, and as she sang the hummingbirds came to do their rounds of the flowers. Later she wasn't able to leave her room anymore, but very occasionally, she would ask for her guitar, and sing a song. If my father was there, she always sang him the same one, by Piero, which starts like this: 'My old man's a good guy [...]' And if he wasn't, she sang songs from her group, the Cuarteto Ellas, or songs by Cat Stevens, the Carpenters, the Beatles or Elton John. Until one day Marta asked for her guitar, tried to sing, and her voice didn't come out. And she said to my mother, with a sad smile in her eyes:

'Oh Mamá, I don't think I'll ever sing again.'

And she never did sing again, because her voice had stopped working.

One day she stopped seeing clearly. 'Daddy, I can't see anything,' she said, 'only light and shadows moving on the ceiling. I think I'm going blind.' That's how she said it, no drama, no tears, just those exact words. My mother says she ran out of the room petrified, knelt down on the living room floor and asked Saint Lucia for a miracle, just one favour, that if she really must take Marta, fine, but please don't make her go blind. The next day Marta could see again and since she died on 13 December, Saint Lucia's day, my mother never doubted this small miracle. Even in the deepest pain, human beings can find relief in small comforts.

Incurable diseases take us back to a primitive state of mind and return us to a magical way of thinking. Since we don't really understand cancer, and can't treat it (much less so in 1972, when Marta died), we attribute its sudden incomprehensible appearance to supernatural forces. We take refuge in superstitious, religious ideas: there is an evil God, or a demon, who is sending us a punishment in the form of a foreign body: something that invades the body and destroys it. Then we offer sacrifices to this deity, we make it promises (giving up smoking, walking on our knees to Girardota and kissing the wounds of the miraculous Christ, buying a golden crown set with precious stones for the Virgin), we recite prayers, we humiliate ourselves in the midst of our requests. The disease being dark, we believe that only something even darker will cure it. That, at least, is what some people in my family believed. And in despair, they clutched at any possibility. There was a medium in Belén who had performed miraculous cures: bring her in. An Amazonian shaman had worked wonders with a concoction made of roots: let Marta drink it. Some nun or priest is in direct communication with the Lord and He hears their pleas: let them come and pray and we will give them alms. It wasn't just the drug from Washington that was tried out in my house; everything was tried, from witches to bioenergetics, religious rituals of all kinds, and not ruling out Extreme Unction. They tried everything, though in desperation rather than distrust, but none of it did any good. My father, obviously, didn't believe in this magic, but he let the other members of the family try whatever they wanted, as long as the treatments they suggested weren't harmful or irritating for Marta. He knew very well what was happening and what was going to happen, and even Dr. Borrero, the specialist who saw my sister, had been saying it since August, with a brutality that was really generous, because at least he didn't create false expectations: 'The child will be dead by December; there's nothing you can do.'

Every day except weekends, when night fell, my father's sister Aunt Inés came over. Sometimes she came in the morning too. A widow and a real saint, as they say, she was a sweet-natured, discreet woman, affectionate without being clingy, who had devoted herself, simply and whole-heartedly, to doing good for others. After Marta came back from the United States, she cared for her every weekday night without fail, with a break only on Saturday and Sunday nights, when my older sisters, Maryluz and Clara, who had come back from Morgantown in November, took turns looking after her. My sisters got thinner and thinner at the same time as Marta, and in the end they weighed almost as little as she did: Clara was down to seventy-seven pounds and Maryluz to seventy-nine, while my father reacted the opposite way and went up two shirt sizes and one suit size in three months, since he never stopped eating and ended up as round as a barrel.

Marta enjoyed Aunt Inés's company, because she knew how to treat ill people, and didn't speak much. If my sister couldn't sleep at night, and wanted company, my aunt would talk to her. She told her, for instance, the story of her husband, Olmedo, who had died while fleeing from Conservative Party hit men, who wanted to kill him just for being a Liberal, and the story of her brother-in-law, Nelson Mora, my father's best friend, who had been murdered by the same hit men, in the north of the Cauca Valley, near Sevilla. Aunt Inés had been happy for a very few years, but had managed to have two children, Lyda and Raúl. As she sat with her and sewed, she thought God had given her more than Marta, who had only ever had two boyfriends, Andrés Posada and Hernán Darío Cadavid, but no husband or children. Marta would ask her about them, because at this stage she wasn't sure which of the two she should love, as she liked them both equally, Andrés because he was a great musician, and Hernán Darío because he was so handsome. Until finally she stopped making things difficult for herself and decided to love them both.

Andrés and Hernán Darío came to the house every day, at different times, at first, Andrés in the morning and Hernán Darío in the evening, until finally, for the last month, they came at the same time, and one held her right hand, and the other her left. Andrés sang her songs by Serrat. Hernán Darío made her laugh. My sister explained to Aunt Inés, who was a little surprised by this scenario, although she thought it lovely, how she loved both of them. One night, while my aunt was sewing the tablecloth that she and my sisters embroidered during those months of vigil, and which she still treasures, Marta explained that Andrés was her soul mate, her spiritual love, and Hernán Darío was her physical companion, her passionate love, that's how my aunt remembers it, and that she liked having them both. It was as if Marta had read Plato's dialogue on love, which my father was so fond of, and which, one day years later, he read aloud to me, the one about the two goddesses of love, Pandemos and Urania, both ever present in our deepest psyche, in this already formatted soul we bring into the world when we're born, thanks to which we all understand each other, and because of which all knowledge has something of the quality of an imperfect memory.

One Sunday night, my sister Maryluz was sitting with Marta through the early hours, as she did every Sunday night. Maryluz was very young; she had left school to marry Fernando without finishing her final year. Though only twenty, she already had a son, Juanchi, who was my father's eldest grandchild and his latest object of adoration, his one source of happiness and main consolation in those months of tribulation. Ten months after our sister's death she had a daughter, named Marta Cecilia in her memory, and who inherited as if by magic her cheerful, sweet nature. After his daughter's death, my father showered his grandchildren with all this huge, lost love, spending whole days and nights with them, writing poems to them and articles about them, describing his love for them as something superior to love itself, and in such impassioned terms they were almost corny. But that Sunday, before dawn, my sister woke up feeling terrible, nauseous, and threw up over the sheets. Maryluz was alarmed by the sight of the vomit and ran out to wake my father: 'Oh Daddy, Daddy, come quickly, come here, Marta's vomited up her liver!'

My father laughed, maybe for the first time in many months.

'Darling, that's impossible, you can't vomit your liver.'

'Yes, Daddy, yes, come and you'll see, I've got it here,' cried Maryluz.

My older sister had put the 'liver' into a white, metallic receptacle, where the sterilized syringes were kept. It was a red, porous mass, the size of a fist. What had happened was that in the last few days, all Marta could eat was watermelon. We didn't give her any food that wasn't watermelon, because everything else went right through her. Every week our relatives in Cartagena, Uncle Rafa and Aunt Mona, sent us heaps of watermelons (which they called *patillas* up on the coast) so Marta could eat the best ones in the country. And what she had vomited was a chunk of watermelon, which looked like liver. It was maybe the only time in those months we were able to laugh, at Maryluz's innocence, who though she was already a married woman, with a child at her side, was still a little twenty-year-old girl.

The watermelons didn't come on their own, but arrived every Friday with my cousin Nora, who was the same age as Marta, and her best friend, and every Friday my aunt and uncle put her on a plane so she could spend the weekend with her. 'I'm sending you the best I've got,' said Uncle Rafa to my mother, and Nora turned up with a change of clothes and the box of *patillas*. Many of Marta's friends were thoughtful like that. As my sister had said that her favourite flowers were red roses (the ones my father would grow for the next twenty years, as if in private communion with his dead daughter), several people brought her one each day: Clara Emma Olarte, one of her classmates, and also her two 'mothers-in-law,' María Eugenia Posada, Andrés' mother, and Raquel Cadavid, Hernán Darío's mother.

29

Marta's vision started to go at the beginning of December. The neurologist said the cancer had now spread to her brain, and that probably one of the growths, at some point, had obstructed some of the synapses in her optic nerve, but that luckily, somehow, the connections had been restored by some other route. She died on the thirteenth, at nightfall, and those last two weeks were spent in great pain, convulsions, and discomfort. My sister, however, never spoke of death, did not want to die or think she was going to. Her discomfort, the fever and pains, she believed, were her body's way of healing itself. When she had attacks of tachycardia she was scared, and asked to be taken to the clinic, so she wouldn't die. Afterwards she asked my aunt for confirmation that this disease, being a disease of the skin, was superficial, and therefore curable. My aunt, just like my father and mother, told her it was, of course it was, even though they were all dying inside as they told her.

When Marta's death throes began my father called all

my sisters and me together for a meeting, in his study, and told each of us a lie. He told Maryluz that since she was the oldest, and already had a one-year-old baby, it would have been more tragic if she had died; he said the same to Clara, because she was already married and had started a family; he nearly didn't know what to say to Eva, except that she mattered more to my mother than Marta; me, because I was the only boy, and Sol, because she was the youngest. And so, for all these reasons, we should consider ourselves lucky, and be very strong, because the family had survived, and we would get over this. Marta, he told us, would be the most beautiful legend in our family history. I think it was a meeting full of useless lies and invented consolations, and he should never have called it.

My father and mother were in her bedroom on the day of her death, as well as Aunt Inés, Hernán Darío, who had had his hair cut that day (and Marta always said that freshly shorn men brought bad luck), and Dr. Jaime Borrero, who had come to see her every day for six months, without charging a cent, not doing a thing but trying to ease her suffering, and ours. He always used to say to me: 'You have to be strong, and help your father, because he's devastated. Be strong and help him.' I nodded, but I didn't know how to be strong, much less how I could help my father. The only thing my father did was to give morphine to my sister, more and more of it. Apart from this, and pampering and encouraging her, there was nothing he could do, except watch as she slowly slipped away, day by day, night after night. The drug lent a serene smile to my sister's face, but each day she needed more to feel well for a few hours. There was no part of her body left where she hadn't been injected, her arms and legs were masses of red puncture marks, as if she'd been eaten alive by ants. My father was always looking for somewhere to give her an injection, and made sure his hands were surgically sterile, as the needles had to be as well, boiled for hours, to prevent infection. Back then, disposable syringes were not yet available.

This last evening, when Dr. Borrero said that Marta was dying, and authorized my father to give her more morphine, a very high dose, so she wouldn't suffer, something almost absurd happened. None of the needles had been boiled sufficiently, and my father grew furious with my mother, and with Aunt Inés, and roared because there wasn't a disinfected needle to give his daughter some morphine, damn it, until Dr. Borrero had to say very softly, but firmly, 'Héctor, that doesn't matter now.' And for the first and last time in those three months of morphine my father committed the offence of giving my sister an injection without sterilizing the syringe or the needle. When the liquid entered her body, my sister, without a word, without opening her eyes, without convulsions or any sound at all, stopped breathing. And my father and mother, at last, after six months of holding back, could break down and cry in front of her. And they cried and cried and cried. And still today, if my father were alive, he would cry at the memory, just as my mother hasn't stopped crying, or any one of us, whenever we think of it, because life, after experiences like this, is nothing but an absurd and senseless tragedy for which there is no consolation.

30

'Hallelujah, Hallelujah, Hallelujah!' A thunderous voice came from the pulpit, the microphone and amplifiers filling every alcove in the church with this one word, over and over, sometimes alternating the Spanish with Latin: 'Alegría, Aleluya, Alegría!' The voice belonged to one of my mother's first cousins, the bishop of Santa Rosa de Osos, Joaquín García Ordóñez. This is how he meant to bid farewell to Marta, apparently with great joy because her soul had now arrived in the kingdom of heaven, and there was much rejoicing in the afterlife, he could see it, because Marta would join the angels and the saints singing the praises of the Lord. He shouted 'Hallelujah, Hallelujah, Hallelujah!' before a church full of people who could only weep as they listened to this deliriously happy bishop, dressed in his most luxurious trappings, in reds, greens and purples, more than incredulous, astonished. 'Alegría, Alegría, Alegría! Sometimes God hurts us by taking away what we love most, to remind us how much we owe Him. Alegría, Aleluya, Alegría.'

At that point in the sermon my father murmured to me, 'I can't take any more, I'm going outside for a while,' and while the monsignor explained why he was so happy (I wonder if his happiness wasn't sincere, and caused precisely by the joy of seeing us suffering so much), my father and I left the nave of the church of Santa Teresita, in Laureles, and stayed outside for a while, in the sun, beneath the blue indifference of heaven, on one of those radiant December days, radiant like García Ordóñez, not speaking, not hearing the bishop's words, until the three girls of the Cuarteto Ellas started to sing their group's sweet songs during communion, and we went back in, to feel the only consolation one can find in sadness, which is to sink further into sadness, until one can bear it no more.

Marta's devastating death is the dividing line between my family's past and present: the future would never be the same for any of us. It was no longer possible for anyone to go back to being fully happy, not even for a short time, because the very instant we looked around at each other in a time of happiness, we knew that someone was missing, that we were incomplete, and had no right to be happy, because plenitude was no longer possible. Even a clear summer sky would always have a black cloud, somewhere on the horizon.

Years later I found out that after this date my father and mother never made love again, as if this source of happiness, too, had been forever denied them. They were still very affectionate towards each other, undoubtedly, some Sunday mornings when they lingered in bed, and we often saw them in a warm, fraternal embrace, but what we couldn't then see was that full intimacy had been lost forever with Marta's death.

On January 29, 2006, I have lunch, as I do almost every

Sunday, with my mother. As we eat our soup in silence, she comes out with this:

'Marta turns fifty today.'

My mother still keeps count of her birthdays. My sister was never older than sixteen (there was one long month to go before she turned seventeen) two years younger than my own daughter, in fact, but my mother still says: 'Marta turns fifty today.' And I remember the little gilded engraving my father had made for the doctors and relatives who looked after her during her illness (Borrero, Echavarría, Inés and Eduardo Abad), as a thank you. It read: 'It is not death that takes away those we love. On the contrary, it keeps them and fixes them in their adorable youth. It is not death that destroys love, but life.' Marta was fixed in her youth and constant in love, and that day, in silence, my mother and I celebrated her fiftieth birthday without candles or ice cream, that dead little girl whom my father, to console himself, said had never existed at all, and was only a beautiful legend.

31

Fifteen years later, in that same church of Santa Teresita, we had to attend another tumultuous funeral. It was 26 August, and the previous night my father had been killed. We held the wake in my older sister Maryluz's house in the last few hours of the night, after going to that morgue from my childhood (the very place he had taken me to see a dead body, as if he had deliberately wanted to prepare me for the future), in the early hours of the morning, to collect his body. In the morning, as usually happens in this country of daily catastrophes, several radio stations wanted to talk to a member of the family. The only one calm enough was my older sister. While they interviewed her, a few officials (the mayor, the governor, a senator) offered their condolences over the airwaves. Then they put the archbishop of Medellín, Monsignor Alfonso López Trujillo, on the line. He told my sister how much he regretted this tragedy and recommended Christian resignation. My sister, who is very Catholic, thanked him on air.

But just a few hours later, at around ten in the morning, we received a telephone call from Santa Teresita, my mother and sisters' parish church, telling us the Requiem scheduled for three o'clock wouldn't be possible. Cardinal López Trujillo had called explicitly to forbid the church from allowing it, in view of the fact that my father was not a believer and never went to Mass either there or anywhere else. It made no sense, the archbishop said, to perform a religious ceremony for someone who had publicly declared himself an atheist and a communist. This was not actually true, as in the rare professions of faith he did make, as contradictory as it might sound, my father always declared himself, as I have mentioned, 'Christian in religion, Marxist in economics and a Liberal in politics.'

The funeral mass was to be presided over by my uncle Javier, my father's brother, and he had come from Cali to celebrate it and be with us. When he found out about the cardinal's order, my uncle went straight to the church and started arguing with the parish priest. He said he would personally assume all responsibility before the archbishop, but it would be a disgrace to withdraw this comfort from the family. It was enough for Javier that my mother and sisters, all practising Catholics, wanted this ceremony and this funeral. A religious burial is not for the dead person, but for his immediate family and relatives, and so his beliefs matter little if those who survive prefer to have a certain kind of funeral for him.

It's true that it may be insulting to an atheist to be forced to attend (in a manner of speaking) a funeral mass, and I wouldn't want one for myself. But first of all, my father didn't know whether he believed or not, and what's more, it was cruel and insulting to deny this comfort—irrational and illusory as it might be—to a

God-fearing widow who only wants to alleviate her suffering with hope for a new life. The cardinal, with his pitiless order, seemed to be pronouncing the words of Creon who wanted to leave Antigone's brother unburied: 'Once an enemy, never a friend, not even after death.' And my uncle, my father's brother, seemed to speak the words of Antigone, Polynices's sister: 'I was not born to impart hatred, but love.'

I didn't know any of this until several days later, when I saw the letter of protest my mother was writing to López Trujillo, and when I read it I repeated out loud once more the word that always comes into my head when I think of this cardinal, now president of the Pontifical Council for the Family in Rome, the word that suits him best, and which I won't repeat here on the advice of my editor to avoid being sued for libel (though not for slander). The parish priest, though frightened, agreed to turn a blind eye, and opened the doors of the church so my uncle could say Mass, and so the thousands and thousands of mourners could come and pay tribute to my father. There was quite a crowd as my family and many other people had announced the service on the radio, and most people in the city had been upset by the murder, though a few may have been pleased. The priest did impose one condition, which was that at least no music should be played, as a sung Mass would be an excessive tribute to the deceased. My uncle Javier didn't answer him, but when the university choir and several musicians began to play and sing, more or less spontaneously, he didn't stop them. His sermon, delivered in floods of tears, was sad and beautiful. He spoke of his brother's martyrdom, of how he'd given his life to defend his convictions, and made the extreme sacrifice because of a deep sense of human compassion and his disgust at injustice. He stated, convinced of the truth of his words, that this just man would not be condemned in the next life, as he had been by some people here on Earth. This time there were no cries of *Alegría, Aleluya*, just murmurs and words choked with emotion trying to express the profound sadness we all felt. This act of bravery, this hint of rebellion, in an Opus Dei priest, is something we will always thank Uncle Javier for. And my mother and sisters were consoled by the hope, so alien to me, that supernatural justice would be done in the next world, as a reward for his good works, and for a possible reunion in another life. I didn't feel this comfort and never can, but I respect it as something as deep-rooted and natural in my family as a good appetite, or pride in all the things my father did during his time in the world.

32

I don't know at what point the thirst for justice crosses the dangerous line beyond which it becomes also a temptation to martyrdom. A highly elevated moral sense always runs the risk of getting out of control and succumbing to a frenzied elation and activism. Exaggerated optimism and confidence in the essential goodness of humankind, untempered by the scepticism of one who has a deeper understanding of the inescapable meanness of spirit human nature hides, leads one to believe it is possible to build paradise here on earth, with the 'good will' of the vast majority. Some fanatical reformers like Savonarola, Bruno or Robespierre can, in spite of themselves, do more harm than good, and Marcus Aurelius thought that the Christians—the madmen of the cross—were wrong to go to the extreme of sacrifice for an abstract notion of truth and justice.

I'm certain my father was not tempted towards martyrdom before Marta's death, but after this family tragedy all problems seemed small, and no price seemed as great as before. After great calamity one's own problems undergo a process of shrinkage, of miniaturization: nobody gives a damn if his finger is chopped off or his car stolen after one of his children has died. When one carries a boundless sadness inside, to die is no longer so serious. Even if one is not actually suicidal, or is unable to raise one's hand against oneself, if the joy of living has been lost, the option of letting oneself be killed, especially for a just cause, becomes more attractive.

My father's excessive love for his children, his exaggerated love for me, led him, a few years after my sister's death, to involve himself to the point of madness in impossible battles and desperate causes. I remember for instance the case of a boy who had disappeared—Doña Fabiola Lalinde's son, who was nearly the same age as me—in which he involved himself with the avenging tenacity of a father. My father found it intolerable that no one would help this mother searching for her son, so close in age to his own son, without any support, with only the strength of her love, her sadness and her desperation.

Compassion is largely a quality of the imagination: it consists of the ability to put oneself in another's place, to imagine what we would feel if we were suffering the same situation. It has always seemed to me that merciless people lack a literary imagination—the capacity great novels give us for putting ourselves in another's place—and are incapable of seeing that life has many twists and turns and that at any given moment we could find ourselves in someone else's shoes,: suffering pain, poverty, oppression, injustice or torture. If my father felt compassion for Doña Fabiola and her disappeared son, it was because he was more than able to imagine what he would feel if he were in a similar situation, with me or one of my sisters in that misty, ambiguous place occupied by the disappeared, with no news, no word, without even the certainty and resignation a dead body allows. To be responsible for someone's disappearance is a crime as serious as kidnapping or murder, perhaps even more awful, causing as it does uncertainty and fear and vain hope.

After my sister's death my father's sense of social duty became stronger and clearer. His passion for justice grew and he ceased altogether to be wary or take precautions, especially, I think, when my younger sister and I went to university and he considered his part in our upbringing complete. 'If they kill me for what I do, would it not be a beautiful death?' my father wondered when someone in the family told him he was exposing himself too much with his denunciations of torture, kidnappings, murder or unjust detentions, which was what he devoted himself to in the last years of his life, as a defender of human rights. But he wouldn't give up his denunciations because of our fears, and he was sure he was doing what he had to do. As Leopardi said: 'One must have a great deal of self-esteem to be able to sacrifice oneself.'

The first struggle he embarked upon after Marta's death was with the Association of Professors of the University of Antioquia, of which he was president, and from where he led a teachers' strike, backed by the students, in defence of his position and against a sly, reactionary rector, Luis Fernando Duque. Duque was a former student of my father's in the same specialism, public health, and for a time supposedly a friend, though he later became a bitter, almost hateful enemy and opponent.

This was towards the end of 1973 and the beginning of

1974 (Marta had died in December 1972), during one of those cyclical crises public universities go through in Colombia. The President of the Association, in 1973, was Carlos Gaviria, a young law professor who from that point became a close friend of our family. That year, during a confrontation between the students and the army, which had occupied the campus on the rector's orders, soldiers had killed Luis Fernando Barrientos, a student, and this death resulted in a riot. The angry students occupied the rectory building, left the body of the dead student, which they had carried on their shoulders throughout campus, on the rector's desk, and then set fire to the university's administrative offices.

Carlos Gaviria, as President of the Professors' Association, wrote a letter that would lead to accusations of incendiary rabble-rousing for the rest of his life, but which had a very clear argument and aim. His thesis was that, in the midst of a whole series of irrational acts, the students had done something irrational, burning down the building, but that the most irrational act of all had been not this, but rather the murder of the student, which seemed to him even worse, and for which all blame lay with the reactionary rector, Duque, who wanted to impose his authoritarian approach on the university, dismissing liberal professors and expecting the army to patrol the campus day and night.

A few months later my father took over from Carlos as President of the Professors' Association, which found itself up against the new professorial statute unilaterally decreed by Duque, who had taken advantage of a national state of siege to impose it, and through which any professional and academic stability for the teaching staff was completely removed. According to the new statute, the rector and deans could dismiss professors under any pretext, and, worse, they started using it, claiming academic or disciplinary motives, to dismiss all the progressive professors. Academic freedom disappeared, and the content of the professors' classes was ideologically monitored by means of regular, unannounced visits to their classrooms.

The army was still occupying the university, and the members of the Association refused to give classes in the presence of the armed forces. Luis Fernando Vélez, an anthropology professor, and also a member of the board of the Association, once said that he refused to give classes not only in the presence of the National Army, but also in the presence of the National Liberation Army, because in those days the guerrillas were also trying to get onto campus to add to the chaos and disorder.

It was a long struggle, at the end of Misael Pastrana's government, and for a while it seemed as though the rector would win it. More than two hundred professors, with Carlos and my father at the top of the list, were dismissed from their posts because of the strike; but fortunately, this coincided with the coming to power of a Liberal president, López Michelsen. My father, who years before had been an activist in a Liberal splinter group headed by López, the MRL (the Liberal Revolutionary Movement), then had an ally he could rely on at the highest level of government, and in the end it was Duque who was dismissed. For once the professors could declare victory in a long labour dispute. The two hundred professors who had been thrown out into the street were reinstated, among them some of the university's best professors. Academic freedom, which Duque had tried to suppress, was revived that year, although later the Minister for Education made the mistake of increasing university attendance to populist extremes, and the university, in order to meet the needs of the vast number of new students, was filled with poorly trained professors, largely from the belligerent far left, who had no time for academia and who started to see people like Carlos Gaviria and my father as bourgeois, decadent, backwards and conservative, simply because they defended serious study and opposed the physical extermination of exploitative capitalists. For a few years things went from one extreme to another, and the university lost its prestige because several of the best trained academic professors chose to leave to found private universities or joined the ones that already existed, rather than have to put up with these new fanatics, from the worst factions of the left, those closest to violence.

CAR ACCIDENTS

33

The day of my high school graduation—it was November 1976; I had just turned eighteen—I was on my way to school in the car I'd borrowed from home, a yellow Renault 4, and between Calle Envigado and Sabaneta I knocked down a woman: Doña Betsabé. She was coming out of Mass with her mantilla on her head and a missal in her hand. She was saying goodbye to her friends and walking backwards into the road, without looking. I slammed on the brakes. The tyres squealed, the car went into a spin and I tried to get it over to the other side of the road, onto the curb, but I hit this lady full on and she flew up into the air. The bumper hit her first, then she flew back into the windscreen, smashed it into a thousand pieces, briefly entered the space where I was sitting with my cousin Jaime, then ricocheted out again, where her body landed, motionless, on the asphalt. Everyone was shouting, the devout women who were leaving the church with her, passers-by, curious members of the public: 'He's killed her, he's killed her!' A crowd gathered round the body, then started looking at me and pointing menacingly.

I had got out of the car and was leaning over her. 'We have to take her to hospital!' I shouted, 'Help me put her into the car!' But no one helped me, not even my cousin Jaime, who seemed dazed from the impact. A pick-up truck came past. My cousin finally helped me to lift her into the back of the truck. I sat in the back with her, alone, thinking she was dead. A bone, the tibia, had torn through her skin and was sticking out of her calf (just the same as John, the boy in the morgue). The truck sped along beeping its horn, towards Envigado hospital, with the driver waving a red rag out the window so people could see it was an emergency. When the woman arrived she was in shock and they took her to the resuscitation room. I went to talk to the doctors. It was a nightmare. I felt like I'd gone crazy. I couldn't stand the fact I might have killed someone. I identified myself. All the doctors had been students of my father's. They phoned him. He was then the director of Social Security in Medellín. The doctors said: 'The woman is in shock and might die. We're doing all we can to revive and stabilize her, then we'll send her by ambulance to the Medellín Clinic, to intensive care.'

There was another problem, the doctors told my father on the phone: 'Is your son insured with the *cárcel de choferes*?' No, my father said. 'If the woman dies, and he doesn't have this special insurance, they'll put him in Bellavista Jail, in a very dangerous block, and anything could happen to him there. He's got some cuts on his arm ... We could hospitalize him while you get him insured. It'll take a couple of days.' My father agreed, and told them to ask me where I wanted to be hospitalized, in order to avoid being taken to Bellavista. He didn't even want to speak to me, he was furious, and for good reason, as he was always telling me I drove too fast. Not thinking, or rather thinking about how I was feeling at that moment, as if I was going mad, I said: 'In the mental hospital.' And my father, who nearly always gave in to whatever I thought I wanted, said, 'Fine.' Then the doctors stitched up the cut on my wrist from the windscreen glass, and wrapped some gauze around it. Doña Betsabé was no longer in shock; she was stable, on a drip-feed, with antibiotics and painkillers, and they put her in an ambulance that sped off towards the centre of Medellín with sirens wailing. 'I think she'll be all right,' the emergency doctor said. 'As well as the puncture wound on her leg—the broken tibia and fibula—her arm, clavicle and several ribs are broken, but it doesn't look like there's any damage to the internal organs, or the head. Let's hope not.'

I was taken to Bello Mental Hospital, in another car. When I got there they handed me over to the attendants. They didn't tell them why I was being admitted. Seeing the bandage on my wrist, they decided it must be a suicide attempt. They asked me what month it was, what year, what day of the week, the names of my grandparents, uncles, aunts and great-grandparents. I was confused, and couldn't remember anything. I kept seeing the accident over and over again like a film, Doña Betsabé flying through the air, the screech of the brakes, her body like a grey whale entering the car through the windscreen and leaving again, her bones broken by the impact. This recurring image was driving me genuinely mad.

They put me in a room with three other real madmen, and I started to feel the same as them. I cried silently. I saw Doña Betsabé; I thought of the graduation ceremony

I wouldn't be able to go to; the presentation of the certificates. Doña Betsabé was in my head like an interminable nightmare, and I was a criminal, a murderer, a delinquent at the wheel. There was a madman who kept repeating the same thing over and over, out loud: 'I've got some cousins who grow bananas in Apartadó, I've got some cousins who grow bananas in Apartadó, I've got some cousins who grow bananas in Apartadó, I've got some cousins who grow bananas in Apartadó.' I had a phrase droning over and over in my head too: I've just killed a woman. Another of the madmen in my room had a collection of illustrated Jules Verne books, and wanted to look at them with me. He smiled suggestively, and balanced the books on my knees. The third man was looking out of the window, motionless, without saying a word or moving a muscle, his gaze vacant and fixed on a point in the distance, transfixed. I felt I would truly go mad from being with them. It began to get dark and I'd had absolutely no news of the outside world, what was happening, whether Doña Betsabé was alive or dead. This horrific prison began to become my world. I started to shout for the attendants: 'I want to call home! I want to know if the woman's alive! I want to use the phone! If you don't get me out of here I really am going to go mad! If I don't get out of here I'm really going to go mad!' There is no better place to go out of your mind than a mental hospital. The most sane and sensible person who is put in a mental hospital will go mad within a few days, even a few hours. The mad people from other rooms came to listen to my shouts, my delirium, and made fun of me: 'This guy's really ill,' they said, 'calm him down, you've got to calm him down.' And they all clapped in unison to alert the attendants, as if they were watching flamenco.

And they came, dressed in dark green, with their attendants' uniforms. Three of them managed to grab me, pulled my trousers down and gave me a long, heavy injection in my buttocks. I don't want to describe the effect this drug had on me. I saw Doña Betsabé, I saw her blood, I saw my bloodied hands, I saw her bones being crushed, I saw my madness, all the images at the same time, unable to focus on anything, my mind invaded by disjointed memories, terrible images that lasted no time at all because another would arrive to take its place. I don't know how long it lasted. I think I fell asleep. In the morning, when I woke up, I said to myself, I must be a model patient. I'm going to be very calm and try and get them to let me phone home. I looked around, at the guy looking at the Jules Verne books, the other one with his gaze lost in space, the one over there droning the same phrase over and over: 'I've got some cousins who grow bananas in Apartadó, I've got some cousins who grow bananas in Apartadó, I've got some cousins who grow bananas in Apartadó, I've got some cousins who grow bananas in Apartadó.' I had a good idea. I found my wallet: I had money.

'Listen, I know it's hard from here, but I need to make a phone call, just one. Here'—I gave the attendant everything I had—'I think this will help you get me permission to use a phone.' He took the cash eagerly and walked off, returning after a while: 'Come on then.' The attendant took me to a payphone, in a corridor, and gave me a coin. I dialled the number of my house, which I hadn't forgotten, which I haven't forgotten even now, thirty years later, even though the house doesn't exist anymore, and there are no longer six-digit telephone numbers in Medellín: 437208. My sister Vicky answered. 'If you don't get me out of this place today, right now, I'm going to go mad for real and I'll never get better. Come and get me quickly, run, now, right now, even if they put me in jail.' I was crying and I hung up. Vicky swore they would get me out. One or two hours later, eternal hours during which my cellmates tried everything to turn me into one of them, the attendants came for me. The psychiatrist made me sign a form that said I was leaving of my own free will and exonerated the mental hospital of all responsibility.

Doña Betsabé was recovering, although it would be months before she was completely better. My mother gave her unemployed children jobs as porters or cleaners in some of her buildings. My father also found work for a few of them. They were very poor and Doña Betsabé kept saying something terrible, really sad, and which shines a revealing light on our society: 'This accident has been a blessing for me. I thank the Lord for it. He sent it, because I was coming out of Mass, and I'd been asking Him to give my children work. But first I had to pay for my sins. I paid for my sins and the Lord gave them work. It's a blessing.' I went to see her once and then didn't want to ever see her again. When I saw her I pictured her as a ghost, her dead body, motionless, which had reacted only once, moaning, when we arrived at Envigado Hospital. If she had died … I don't want to even think about it. Maybe I'd still be in Bello Mental Hospital.

'You were going very fast,' my father said. 'The skid marks were really long. This must not happen again.' But, scarcely a year and a half later, it did.

34

At the beginning of 1978 my father and I went, on our own, to Mexico City. At the request of the ambassador, María Elena de Crovo, President López Michelsen had appointed my father Cultural Attaché at the Colombian Embassy in Mexico. I had just turned nineteen and it was the first time I'd had a passport (an official passport) and the first time I'd left the country. I took my first international flight; for the first time I was given a little tray of hot food on a plane. It all seemed very grand, important and wonderful, and the five-hour journey seemed to me like an amazing feat. In Mexico City we lived, at first, in a boarding house, a sort of hotel-apartment, in the suburb of Colonia Roma, where our beds were made and our clothes washed.

The consul was a kind man, a nephew of the former president, Turbay Ayala. The ambassador had spent a turbulent time as Minister of Employment (when she'd had to deal with the assassination, at the hands of the left, of the trade union leader José Raquel Mercado, and with a terrible State doctors' strike, with patients dying in emergency rooms, and pregnant women giving birth in the corridors), and was an unhappy woman, perhaps aware that her political career had long ago reached its peak. She considered the Ambassadorship to Mexico not a reward, but a kind of exile, a farewell to political life. Perhaps this was why she drank too much, and had asked my father to take charge of the Embassy's daily routine and cover her back in the office, now that she no longer had any desire to work. My father, who considered her a good friend, did this gladly.

My father and I were an inept pair of housemates and my mother—who had had to stay in Medellín running her business—was not due to arrive for several months. Neither of us knew how to cook and the few times I tried to make breakfast it consisted of hard bread and scorched eggs. We always ate out, and the consul had lent us a red Volkswagen Beetle in which I learned to negotiate the endless, chaotic avenues of the Mexican capital, whose traffic is the most diabolical in the world. A traffic jam on the ring road could last for as long as a plane journey to Colombia. The traffic would stop completely, and one would take out a book to read, while the world kept turning and everything moved, except for the traffic on the ring road. Very early in the morning I would drive my father to the Embassy, in La Zona Rosa, and then I'd have the whole day ahead of me, though I didn't know what to do with it. A friend of my father's came to my rescue, Iván Restrepo (the husband of my father's secretary at the Faculty of Medicine), who had emigrated to Mexico twenty years earlier. Since then, whenever I think of Mexico, I think of Iván Restrepo, and of his house on Calle Amatlán, in Colonia Condesa, where I always stay when I go to Mexico, very near to the house of Fernando Vallejo, another friend I once had and no longer have.

I don't think I've ever read as much as I did in those months in Mexico: in the mornings in Iván's stupendous library, its doors left open for me so I could be alone there, in silence, in the company of his thousands and thousands of books; and in the evenings in the tiny apartment my father and I finally rented, in Colonia Irrigación, on a street called Presa las Pilas, though I no longer remember the number. I only know that above us lived a French diplomat who taught me how to listen to Jacques Brel, and on the roof terrace there were still some hovels where the maids slept. After a few weeks of scorched eggs and instant coffee, Teresa arrived from Colombia, the maid who spent her whole life working for us, and who still goes every Thursday, even though she's retired, to do my younger sister's ironing. Even now, this trip to Mexico is Teresa's main source of pride, and so that no one can doubt this glorious past of hers in 1978, she still uses Mexican idioms, thirty years after having returned. She doesn't say 'a la orden' for 'how can I help you?' like we do here but 'mande'; she doesn't say 'cuidado!' (look out!) but 'aguas!,' and instead of 'vamos!' (let's go), she says 'ándele!' What with Teresa in the house, and diplomatic receptions, my father and I began to eat well again—perhaps better than ever, and for the first time in my life with wine, since my father, being a diplomat, could have it brought to the house tax-free.

Sometimes, very occasionally, I would stay at Iván's house for the 'Angangueo Cultural Association' lunches, which were attended by important people. Writers like Tito Monterroso, Carlos Monsiváis, Elena Poniatowska and Fernando Benítez; painters like Rufino Tamayo, José Luis Cuevas and Vicente Rojo; actresses like Margo Su, who was Iván's secret girlfriend and the best business-woman the popular theatre of Mexico had ever had; great musicians like Pérez Prado; singers and dancers like La Tongolele and Celia Cruz. These lunches lasted the whole afternoon, and consisted of a thousand indigenous dishes from the most sophisticated Mexican gastronomy: green chilli chicken from Xalapa, *huachinangos* from Veracruz (which is the same as our red snapper), breast of *huajalote* (turkey) with *mole poblano* (chilli and chocolate sauce), or white *mole* with pine nuts and spices, all kinds of *tamales*, little fish from Pátzcuaro, *gorditas* with pork and beans, stuffed chillies, octopus in almonds, corn on the cob with coriander ... I remember Benítez always said goodbye to me in the same way: 'Be very happy, young man,' and gave a theatrical bow. When I got outside, this goodbye gave me a sudden attack of laughter and happiness; I had to jump up and down to conceal it. Since then I have tried to follow his advice, without much success.

Nevertheless, I didn't meet the writers whom I most admired and wanted to get to know on that trip: Juan Rulfo, a taciturn man who hardly ever went out; Gabriel García Márquez, who was not of this world; Octavio Paz, all of whose poetry and essays I read in those months, but who had a Pontifical attitude and didn't see anyone unless you requested an audience with him three months in advance; and a younger poet who dazzled me and whom I still love, José Emilio Pacheco, who spent half his time in the United States. Neither Rulfo nor Paz nor Gabo nor Pacheco belonged to the most commendable Angangueo Cultural Association, which was for people who were happier than they were famous, who didn't taken their lives or their vocation or anything too seriously. Maybe one always has to choose in life whether to be happy like Benítez or famous like Paz. If only we were all wise enough to choose the first, like my friend Iván Restrepo, or like Monsiváis and Princess Poniatowska, who are happy rather than famous people, or at least are equally famous and happy.

I was in Mexico for nine months, until October. My father stayed until December, just one year, and what I'd like to emphasize is that he allowed me to spend this whole, shamefully decadent sabbatical without any pressure whatsoever to start university or to work. I just read, enjoyed life and accompanied him in his diplomatic life from time to time. I especially remember that I read, among many other books, the seven volumes of Proust's *À la Recherche du Temps Perdu*, with a passion and a concentration I have perhaps never felt again for any book. If there is one fundamental reading experience in my life, I think it occurred during those months—February, March, April—spent reading the great Proustian saga *En busca del tiempo perdido* in the evenings (in the Alianza edition, the first three volumes translated by Pedro Salinas, and the rest by Consuelo Berges), a period that marked my life forever. It was then that I decided that I wanted to do exactly the same as Proust: spend the hours of my life reading and writing. Two great names set the course of twentieth century literature, Joyce and Proust, and I believe that choosing which to follow is as important to the writer, as it is to a politician to decide whether to be left- or right-wing. Some people find Proust boring and Joyce fascinating; for me it is the exact opposite.

My father had given me permission to do nothing. It was enough for him that I was reading and getting to know a great metropolis, its cinemas and concerts and museums. The other thing I did was to sign up for some literary workshops at the Casa del Lago cultural centre. Poetry with David Huerta, short stories with José de la Colina, and drama with someone I don't remember. In the evenings, once a week, I went to another more private workshop that took place in the Casa de España, with a great teacher from Central America, Felipe San José, of whom I have never heard anything else since. He was a sort of disciple of Rubén Darío, and immensely knowledgeable about literature, and also endlessly generous when commenting on the writing his pupils did. The first contact I had with Spanish Golden Age literature was with him, as well as with the contemporary Spanish novel. They were long months of pleasure, reading, inertia and happiness.

Midway through this year Grandpa Antonio wrote my father an anxious letter. He had discovered that I, pursuing my Proustian ideal of life, spent my days lying in bed, or on a divan, reading endless novels and sipping sweet Sauternes wine, as if I were an old maid withdrawn from the world, an Oblomov of the tropics, or a mincing nineteenth-century dandy. Nothing could be more alarming to him, with his ideas on the formation of his grandson's personality and future—and seen from the outside, through the eyes of an active, pragmatic cattle farmer, or even with my own eyes now, I have to acknowledge that it must have looked slightly aberrant, and that maybe Grandpa was right. But as always when it came to any criticism of me, when my father read this letter, he only laughed out loud and commented that Grandfather didn't understand that I was putting myself through university at my own expense. Where did he get this confidence in me, which survived even these appalling symptoms of indolence?

In March we took the first of several trips to the United

States, in a super-luxurious BMW, lent to us by the consul. It was the first time I had entered this great country, and we did so via Laredo, on the borders of Texas. We were going to visit two of my father's students, one in San Antonio, Héctor Alviar, an anaesthetist, and the other in Houston, Óscar Domínguez, a plastic surgeon. We were also going to buy a car tax-free since my father was allowed to do this, as a diplomat. We bought a huge Lincoln Continental, with all sorts of luxuries we'd never seen before: automatic gearshift, electric windows, air conditioning, seats and wing mirrors that moved at the press of a button, and an enormous engine that guzzled gas like a drunk guzzles bottles of mescal. Aged nineteen, with the androgynous appearance of an adolescent who is only slowly maturing, who is still almost a child, a languid, voluptuous youth, I remember how I cruised along in that great white car, along the paths of Chapultepec Park, on the way to the Casa del Lago, where I took my unhurried literature courses. I felt like Proust in the latest model luxury cabriolet, on his way to visit the Duchess of Guermantes and en route discussing cattleya orchids with Odette de Crécy. Apart from one girl who once took me to the home of her parents, extremely wealthy industrialists who lived in Polanco, if I'm not mistaken, I don't remember a single one of my classmates from those courses; but it's clear we weren't spending our time cultivating cattleya. Perhaps I can remember two more people. There was a very beautiful student, at the Casa de España, a woman of about thirty, who was professor San José's lover. And a very intelligent *mestizo* student, who was writing a historical novel filled with poetry about the Texcoco Indians at the time of the arrival of Hernán Cortés. On the last day of the course, as I said goodbye because I was going back to Colombia, I remember he said: 'Héctor, let me say something very seriously, please: never stop writing.' This request, to me, seemed very strange, as it was like suggesting I never stop living. Since then, and although it was more than ten years before I published my first book, I have never had the slightest doubt about what I wanted to do with my life. In Mexico I wrote the story with which, a year later, I would win a national competition: *Stones of Silence*. I think I owe a debt of gratitude to José de la Colina and Felipe San José for the corrections that improved it. And to David Huerta, the son of Efraín, I owe my final abandonment of poetry, the genre I believed I was most suited to, but for which it seems I have no gift, and since then, whenever I come up with a hendecasyllable or an alexandrine, I have always chosen, instead of thrusting it into the limelight, rather to conceal it within a paragraph of prose.

But this year of excessive closeness with my father was also the year I realized I had to move away from him, even if it meant killing him. I don't want this to sound overly Freudian: I mean it literally. A father as perfect as he was can become unbearable. Even though he thinks everything you do is fine (or rather, *because* he thinks everything you do is fine), there comes a time when a confused, insane mental process drives you to no longer want this ideal god to be always there to tell you okay, fine, yes, as you wish. It is as if, in the last stages of adolescence, one doesn't need an ally, but an antagonist. But it was impossible to fight with my father, and so the only way of confronting him was to make him disappear, even if I too died in the attempt.

I think I only really freed myself from him, from his excessive love and his perfect way of treating me, when I went to live in Italy with Bárbara, my first companion, the mother of my two children, in 1982. But the climax of total dependence and communion with him was in Mexico, aged nineteen, in 1978, when as I say I wanted to kill him, kill him and kill myself, and I'm going to describe it very briefly, since it's a memory I don't like to recall, due to how confused, imprecise and embarrassing it is, even though nothing actually happened.

We were driving down a deserted road in the north of the country, on our way back from one of our trips to Texas, in an old, powerful car (the first one was stolen a few weeks after we got it to Mexico City), a big car like a hearse, which Óscar Domínguez, my father's student, had lent us to replace the stolen Lincoln. It was a huge desert, beautiful in its desolation. I felt a kind of suicidal impulse and accelerated without thinking. I pushed the powerful old heap of junk, a Cadillac, up to 80, 100, 120 miles an hour. The car roared and shook; its ancient bodywork vibrated like a rocket about to shoot up from the ground, and I had the clear sensation we were going to be killed, but I didn't stop pushing the accelerator all the way down, wanting to kill myself. My father was at my side, asleep. It would be an instantaneous death for us both, in the desert. I don't know if that's what I was thinking, but when a herd of goats appeared in the road some metres ahead, I came face to face with death, and slammed on the brakes. I braked and braked and braked, just as I'd braked that time with Doña Betsabé, and the hulking old American car held its course without skidding or flipping over as I braked long and hard, swaying in the middle of a hellish noise, and the goats leapt aside, their great leaps forming dark arcs in the air, and the goatherd shouted and waved his hands around, his arms like the sails of a windmill, but nothing hit us, not a horn or a tail, and the car finally came to a halt unscathed a few metres ahead of the terrified animals. My father woke up startled by the noise and the braking, only just held in place by his seat belt, and without saying a word seemed to understand everything, because he made me swap places, in silence, and although he was a terrible driver, he drove all the way back to Mexico City, at 30 miles an hour, for half a day, without saying a single word.

35

In 1982, a few months after I went to live in Italy for the first time, and shortly before his sixty-first birthday, my father received a short letter from a secretary in the Human Resources department of the University of Antioquia. In it he was instructed in a cold, bureaucratic tone to report to their offices to fill in the paperwork relating to his immediate retirement. He received this totally unexpected news like a blow to the head. His favourite student, Silvia Blair, who had just become a teacher in the faculty, remembers how her former professor came looking for her in the office, his eyes blood-red, crying his heart out (my father cried with no shame for his tears, not like our stoical Spanish sons, but like a Homeric hero), not able to believe that the university where he had studied for seven years and been head of department for a further twenty-five, could throw him out on the street like a dog simply for having turned sixty, and without even thanking him for the work to which he had devoted his entire life, apart from brief interludes abroad. He had been student representative on the Board of Higher Education, had opened the Department of Preventative Medicine, founded the National School of Public Health, taught several generations of healthcare workers, organized strikes to defend the university's teachers, been president of their union several times, and nearly all the doctors in Antioquia had been students of his. Yet suddenly one day, with no consideration for all this, they retired him, threw him out.

In his second book, *Letters from Asia*, written in the Philippines, my father maintained he had become a professor too soon, and that true teachers only attain that stature after many years of maturity and meditation. 'What a great number of mistakes,' he wrote, 'are committed by those of us who attempt to teach without having yet achieved the maturity of spirit and peace of mind experience and greater awareness bring towards the end of our lives. Mere knowledge is not wisdom. Nor is wisdom alone enough. To teach other men, one needs knowledge, wisdom and a good heart. We who became teachers without first being wise men should humbly ask our students for forgiveness for the harm we did them.'

And now, precisely when he felt himself arriving at this stage of life, he was no longer impelled by vanity, and ambition carried less weight, when he was guided less by passion and emotions and more by a mature rationality built of many hardships, they were throwing him out. For him, teaching, unlike sport or beauty or passion, was associated with maturity and wisdom, those things one attains more frequently with age. It's fine for those who wish to retire, but if a teacher has not lost his mental faculties, and has finally understood what is really important in his profession, and if furthermore his students love him, suddenly to prevent him from continuing to teach is a genuine crime and a waste. In Europe, in Asia, in the United States, they don't remove great teachers from their posts when they are old, but rather they take better care of them; they lessen their academic load, but let them stay on, as teachers of teachers, nurturing both students and other professors in their intellectual growth. In fact numerous students protested at his forced retirement, and Silvia Blair wrote a furious letter and gave out thousands of copies, signed by professors and students, saying that a university had little future when it retired its best teachers against their will, just so that it could employ, for less money, three young lecturers, with no experience of the world or of the material they hoped to teach.

Being forcibly pensioned off hurt him a great deal, but he didn't stay bitter for long. He declared, simply, during a brief celebration in his honour that his favourite students arranged, that he was going to live more happily, read more, spend more time with his grandchildren and, above all, devote himself to 'cultivating roses and friends.' And that's what he did. He spent three or four days a week, from Thursday to Sunday, on the farm in Rionegro, in the rose beds every morning, trying out cross breeds, grafting, weeding the beds and pruning the bushes, while in the afternoon he read and listened to classical music, or prepared his radio programme (*Thinking Aloud*, it was called), or wrote his newspaper articles. In the evening he went to visit his soul mate, the poet Carlos Castro Saavedra, and at night he read some more until he was overcome by sleep. The rose beds gradually became full of the most exotic roses, for him and for all of us, a garden of great value, real and symbolic. In the last interview he did, at the end of August 1987, when he was asked about rebellion, he referred to his rose beds: 'Rebellion is something I wouldn't want to give up. I've never been one to get down on my knees. I only ever get down on my knees in front of my roses and I've never got my hands dirty except with the soil from my garden.'

Many of his friends and relations have memories associated with my father's rose beds, which still exist, somewhat beleaguered, on the farm in Rionegro. He didn't give his flowers to just anyone, only to people he thought were good, and sometimes he refused them with a dark smile on his face, and a silence only we could comprehend. On the other hand he would explain everything he could about how he grew them to people he got on well with. 'The female roses are the only ones that flower, but they have thorns. The males don't have thorns, but they never flower,' he would always say, with a smile, as he explained how the grafts were done. He liked showing people every part of the farm's garden, not just the rose beds, but also the orchard, the guava trees with tiny red guavas, the avocado trees that bore fruit the whole year round, because they were planted on top of the septic tank, and the gooseberries, which he peeled and put into our mouths himself. He would pause resentfully in front of the only tree that never flowered, an infertile camellia still in the same place, as if this bush had done him a personal injury: 'Why will it never flower?' It only flowered once: while he was complaining about it to Mónica, Bárbara's sister, he suddenly saw a solitary, unique white camellia. Then he picked it and gave it to her, delighted at this one exception in so many years of life.

He returned to Medellín on Monday mornings, and it

was during these years free of professional commitments that he dedicated all his spare time (when he wasn't spoiling his grandchildren or cultivating roses and friends) to defending human rights, which seemed to him the most pressing medical battle of the time in Colombia. He wanted to apply his dreams of practical justice to what he considered most urgent.

He loved gardening because he felt like he was going back to his family's rural origins. But while he enjoyed this attachment to the countryside and the land, he still had dreams of reforming medicine. He dreamt there could be a new type of doctor, a *poliatrist*, he used to say, a healer of the polis, and he wanted to be an example of how this new doctor-of-society should behave, not concerning himself with attacking and curing disease, case by case, but rather intervening in its deepest and most fundamental causes. It was for this reason that, in his post as head of preventative medicine and public health, he had left the classroom more and more frequently to take his students to look at the city as a whole: the working-class neighbourhoods, the rural districts, the aqueduct, the slaughterhouse, the prisons, the private clinics for the rich, hospitals for the poor, and also the countryside, the large estates, the smallholdings and the living conditions of villagers in rural areas.

Two years after he retired, pressure from students and colleagues led to him being asked to return to the university, though only to give a few seminars, and he accepted the job on the condition that he could teach the majority of his classes, as he had always dreamt of doing, away from the classroom. My younger sister, Sol, who in those years had started to study medicine at a private university, remembers that my father invited her and her classmates to take some courses on '*poliatry*' in

Bellavista prison. My sister suggested it in class, but her classmates opposed the idea. One of them, now a cardiologist, stood up and said, in the most offensive, aggressive tone he could manage: 'We have nothing to learn in a prison.' As he was the leader of the group, all his classmates accepted his verdict, so the only one who took the course was my sister, and she remembers those outings as some of the weeks when she learned most about medicine, although a different kind of medicine, social medicine, in contact with those who were suffering most, and with their particular personal, economic or family complaints.

During these trips out to the country, my father didn't give answers, as usually happens in lessons, but used the old Socratic method of teaching by asking questions. Some students found this disconcerting and even protested: what good was a professor who instead of teaching only asked questions and more questions? If they went to hospital it was not to treat patients, but to question or measure them; it was the same with the villagers. They had to investigate the social causes, the economic and cultural origins of disease: why this malnourished child was in this hospital bed; or how this wound had been caused by a bullet, a car, a machete or a knife; or why certain social groups got tuberculosis, or leishmaniasis or malaria more than others. In prison they studied the origins of violent behaviour, but they also tried to make sure that those with TB weren't kept where they could infect the rest of the inmates, and used alternative programmes (classes, lectures, film screenings) to try to control drug addiction, sexual abuse, the spread of AIDS, and so on.

My father's novel conception of violence as a new type of plague went back a long time. At the first Colombian

Conference on Public Health, which he organized in 1962, he had given a paper that would be a milestone in the country's history of social medicine: his lecture was called *The Epidemiology of Violence*, and in it he insisted that the factors that triggered violence be studied. He proposed, for example, that the personal and family background of violent offenders be scientifically studied; their social integration; their 'cerebral system'; their 'attitudes towards sex and the concepts they have of machismo.' He recommended that 'a complete physical, psychological and social examination of violent offenders be carried out, along with an identical comparative examination of another group of non-violent people, similar in number, age and circumstances, in the same areas and ethnic groups, in order to analyze the differences between the two.'

He carefully observed the most frequent causes of death, and verified the intuitions he had, without figures, just through watching what was happening and listening to what he was told: the cyclical epidemic of violence in Colombia that had gripped the country since time immemorial was growing again, the same violence that had killed his high school friends and taken his grandfathers to the civil war. Here the most harmful thing for human health was not hunger or diarrhoea or malaria or viruses or bacteria or cancer or respiratory or heart disease. The most noxious agent, the one that caused the most deaths among the citizens of the country, was other human beings. And the pestilence caused by this agent, halfway through the 1980s, took its usual form, that of political violence. The State, or more specifically the army, assisted by squadrons of hired killers, the paramilitaries, backed by the security organizations and sometimes by the police as well, was exterminating political opponents on the left, in order to 'save the country from the threat of Communism,' as they claimed.

His final struggle, then, was also a medical struggle, the struggle of a healthcare worker, although one fought outside classrooms and hospitals. A constant and avid reader of statistics (he used to say that without a good census it was impossible to plan any public policy scientifically), my father watched the progress of this new epidemic in terror, an epidemic that in the year of his death registered homicide figures higher than those of a country at war, and which in the first few years of the 1990s led to Colombia attaining the sad distinction of being placed first in the list of the world's most violent countries. It was no longer the diseases he had fought so hard against (typhoid, enteritis, malaria, tuberculosis, polio, yellow fever) that caused most deaths in the country. The cities and the countryside of Colombia were being sprayed with more and more blood from the worst of the diseases suffered by man: violence. And like doctors in earlier times, who contracted bubonic plague, or cholera, in their desperate attempts to combat them, so Héctor Abad Gómez fell too, victim of the worst epidemic, of the most destructive plague a nation can suffer: armed conflict between different political groups, uncontrolled delinquency, terrorist explosions, the settling of scores between mafiosos and drug-traffickers.

Vaccines were of no use in combatting all this: all he could do was to speak, write, condemn, explain how and where the massacre was occurring, and demand that the State, with its monopoly on power, do something to halt the epidemic, while still upholding the rules of democracy, without the high-handedness or brutality that placed it on the same level as the criminals it claimed to be fighting. In the last book published while he was alive, a few months before he was murdered, *Theory and Practice of Public Health*, he writes and emphasizes that freedom of thought and expression is 'a right hard-won through history by thousands of human beings, a right we must preserve. History demonstrates that preserving this right requires constant effort, occasional struggles and even, at times, personal sacrifices. Many professors from this country and from all the places on Earth have been prepared to do this and will continue to be in the future.' And he added a reflection as valid today as it was then:

'The alternative becomes clearer every day: either we behave like intelligent, rational animals, respecting Nature and accelerating as much as possible the process of *humanization* we are only just beginning, or the quality of human life will deteriorate. Some of us are starting to have doubts about the rationality of human groups. But if we do not act rationally, we will suffer the same fate as some cultures and some stupid species of animals, of whose suffering and path to extinction all that remains are fossils. Species that do not change biologically, ecologically or socially when their habitat changes, are bound to perish after a period of indescribable suffering.'

From 1982 until his murder in 1987, he worked tirelessly on the Committee for the Defence of Human Rights of Antioquia, which he chaired. He fought against the new plague of violence using the only weapon he had left: freedom of thought and of expression: words, peaceful demonstrations, publicly denouncing those who violated rights of all kinds. He sent endless, mostly unanswered, letters to officials (the President, the attorney general, ministers, generals, squadron leaders), citing full names and concrete cases. He published articles in which he named torturers and murderers. He condemned every massacre, every kidnapping, every 'disappearance,' every act of torture. He went on silent protest marches with young people and teaching colleagues from the university who believed in the same cause (Carlos Gaviria, Leonardo Betancur, Mauricio García, Luis Fernando Vélez, Jesús María Valle), and participated in forums, conferences and demonstrations all over the country. And his office was filled with hundreds of reports from desperate people who could turn to no one, neither to the courts nor to state officials, but for whom he was the only hope. It is enough to look at these documents, some of which are still in my mother's house, to be at once disgusted and overwhelmed by pain: photos of tortured and murdered people, desperate letters from parents and siblings of kidnapped or missing relatives; from parish priests in distant villages to whom no one listened and who turned to him with their testimonies— and weeks later the news of the murder of those same priests. There are letters written by him in which the death squads are named, with the killers' first and last names, but to which he received in reply only the disdain and indifference of the government, the incomprehension of journalists, and the unjust accusations of some of his newspaper colleagues that he was allied with subversive forces.

He did not, as some said, denounce only the government and close his eyes to the atrocities of the guerrilla war. Looking through his articles and statements it is clear he detested the guerrillas' kidnappings and indiscriminate attacks, and he strongly, even despairingly, denounced them too. But he considered it more serious that the very State that claimed to respect the rule of law was engaged in fighting a dirty war—either directly or vicariously, by hiring thugs (paramilitaries and death squads) to fight on its behalf.

In the year of his death this dirty war was having a devastating effect on public universities. Some agents of the State, along with their accomplices, the paramilitaries, had decided that this was where the seed and the ideological life-blood of subversion lay, and began to carry out vicious attacks and murders. In the months before my father's murder, in his beloved University of Antioquia alone, they had killed seven students and three professors. One might think that faced with these figures, citizens would be alarmed or shaken. But life seemed to go on as normal, and only this 'madman,' this friendly, bald, sixty-five year old professor, with a booming voice and a devastating youthful passion, shouted out the truth and condemned barbarity. 'They are exterminating intelligence, they're disappearing the students with the most enquiring minds, they're killing political opponents, they're murdering the priests who are most committed to their villages and parishes, they're beheading popular leaders in neighbourhoods and villages. The State sees communists and dangerous opponents in any thinking person.' The extermination of the Patriotic Union, a far left political party, happened around this time, eventually claiming four thousand civilian lives across the country.

All around him, in the university where he worked, people were dying, murdered by paramilitary groups. Between July and August of 1987, in a clear campaign of persecution and extermination, they killed the following students and teachers from the University of Antioquia: 4 June, Edisson Castaño Ortega, dentistry student; 14 July, José Sánchez Cuervo, veterinary science student;

26 July, John Jairo Villa, law student; 31 July, Yowaldin Cardeño Cardona, a student at the University High School; 1 August, José Ignacio Londoño Uribe, social and communication studies student; 4 August, anthropology professor Carlos López Bedoya; 6 August, engineering student Gustavo Franco; 14 August, professor in the Faculty of Medicine, and Patriotic Union senator, Pedro Luis Valencia.

Horrific details had emerged about some of these crimes, which my father told us: one of the students, after being tortured and murdered, was tied to a post, and his body ripped apart by a grenade. José Sánchez Cuervo was found with a broken nose, bruises on his waist, one eyeball burst by a blow, several severed fingers, and a bullet hole through his ear. Ignacio (known as Nacho) Londoño had seven bullets in his head and one in his left hand. When they found him, one of the fingers on his right hand had been severed. This young man earned his living as a recreation worker (especially in old people's homes, as he was good with the elderly), and was slowly working his way through a degree in social and communication studies while supporting his 82-year-old father. This old man had to go and collect Ignacio's body in the neighbourhood of Belén high up in a mountainous area of the city, and recognized him because the first thing he saw was his son's hand missing a finger, thrown into the undergrowth. A little further on he found the body, with signs of torture. The boy had been about to graduate, but was suspect to the paramilitaries because he'd been a student for nearly ten years, and this was typical of guerrilla infiltrators, who sat few exams and took few courses, so as to stay in university longer. Londoño didn't have a guerrilla bone in his body, and his father's great joy in life was that in a short time he would have a professional son who would at least be able to 'pay for his funeral.' Instead he had to bury his son, bearing a pain he no longer wished to survive.

In normal people's houses around this time, parents were trying to control their children so they wouldn't take part in protests and demonstrations that might put their lives at risk, but at our house, the opposite was happening. As he was the least conservative of older people to begin with, and with each day that passed became more liberal and more rebellious, the roles were reversed, and it was us children, who tried to stop my father from exposing himself or going out on marches, or writing his stark denunciations, because of the climate of extermination we were living in. Rumours also started to appear that his life was in danger. Jorge Humberto Botero, who moved in the highest circles of the government, told my sister Clara, his ex-wife: 'Tell your father to be more careful, and tell him I know what I'm talking about.' My other sister Eva's husband, Federico Uribe, heard what was being said around the Country Club, and warned her, too: 'Your father is exposing himself too much and he'll end up getting killed.'

There were also indirect signs of a dangerous increase in general hostility from several important people. Eva's sons played polo, as did her husband, so she sometimes went to polo matches at the Llanogrande Club. One day, purely by chance, she happened to sit next to another polo player not nearly as good as my nephews: Fabio Echeverri Correa. He was drunk and berated her in an unpleasant tone of voice: 'I choose who I sit with; and I won't let the daughter of a communist sit down next to me.' Luigi, Echeverri's son, who was always very nice to my family, strongly defended Vicky to his father.

Without a word, my sister got up and changed seats.

My mother was the only one who didn't believe these rumours, ever, not even at the end, and she would get annoyed with the people who spread them: 'What are they thinking, they can't do anything to Héctor!' To her my father was such a good man that no one would ever dare threaten him. Two weeks later, when her husband was dead, even though she was devastated, she tried to go back to work and went to check on 'The Stable,' which was what they called the building where the 'sacred cows' of Medellín lived—that is, its richest industrialists and businessmen. In reality 'The Stable' was and is called the Plaza Building, although now almost all of its occupants have died or moved away. From one moment to the next the pain and sadness became too much and she sat down on the stairs to cry inconsolably. Don José Gutiérrez Gómez was just going into his office. Like Fabio Echeverri, he'd been president of the National Association of Industrialists, and what's more, was its founder. Don Guti went over to my mother, tried to help her up, and my mother said: 'Now I doubt all of you. I wonder whether I've been a naïve and terrible person managing the buildings of the richest people in Medellín. I think the people who gave the order to kill Héctor are among these people, although not you, Don Guti.' Mr. Gutiérrez stayed with her, without saying a word, for a long time, sitting next to her on the stairs.

For my mother, just as for my sisters and I, there remained, and in part still remains, a lingering doubt, difficult to shake off. Who, exactly, was advising Carlos Castaño, and leading the military officers who gave the orders and decided who to kill? We've only been given indirect, general answers: it was banana producers from Urabá; cattle farmers from Puerto Berrío and Magdalena

Medio allied with the paramilitaries; agents from the intelligence service stirred up by far-right politicians; officials harmed by the Human Rights Committee's denunciations ... Only once, one of my nephews, at a huge ranch by the coast, near Magangué, which he visited in the holidays, overheard an explicit confession from a group of paramilitaries who were guarding the ranch. It was the anniversary of his murder and my father appeared briefly on the news on TV.

'That son of a bitch was one of the first we killed in Medellín,' they remarked. 'He was a really dangerous communist; and we should keep an eye on his son, because he's going down the same route.' My nephew, terrified, didn't say that the man they were talking about was his grandfather.

When my sister Maryluz, the eldest, and his favourite daughter, begged my father to stop going on marches because he was going to get killed, he would calm her with kisses and laughter. The marches themselves, however, were for him a deeply serious matter, although he marched enthusiastically, almost happily, when he saw the number of people accompanying him, even if their protest was a futile cry of desperation. He was also naïve. Once, with a group of students, professors and human rights activists, he was marching towards the provincial government, in formation, when suddenly he found himself all alone, without a single fellow marcher, walking along with his placard. All the others had turned back because up ahead there was a van full of riot police, but he kept on walking; when they stopped him and bundled him into the police van, the other people held there asked him why he hadn't turned back in time, like everyone else: he explained that he'd confused the police van with a rubbish truck.

He was also sometimes left on his own when he was giving a speech, something he always did at the end of a march, and would see his terrified audience break up from one moment to the next. Then he would turn around and see an army troop approaching. They never did anything to him, and if they detained him, they let him go straight away, as if shamed by his evident innocence and dignity. Always immaculate, always impeccably dressed in suit and tie, always ingenuous and open and smiling. His best form of self-defence was his long-standing prestige as a good-natured professor, his gentle way of dealing with people, his enormous warmth. He was always putting himself at risk, but nearly everyone thought: they won't do anything to Dr. Abad, they'll never touch him, everyone knows he's a good guy. After all he had been doing the same thing for fifteen years now and they had never touched him. The government always called on him to settle desperate cases: the occupation of a church, a consulate or a factory, the handing over of a guerrilla or a kidnap victim. All sides trusted his word.

On 11 August of that fateful year he wrote a piece entitled *In Defence of Life and Universities*. In it he denounced the murder (and in some cases torture) in the last month of five students and three professors from different faculties, and he explained this attack as follows: 'The University of Antioquia is in the sights of those who want us to question nothing, who want us all to think the same; it is a target for those who believe knowledge and critical thought are a danger to society, and so use terror as a weapon in order that this institution engaged in critical dialogue with society loses its balance, and succumbs to the desperation of those who have been subjugated by learning the hard way.'

Going back through his articles one nearly always finds a very tolerant, balanced person, without any of the dogmatism of the left characteristic of those angry years. There are, nevertheless, a few notes that, read today, might seem exaggerated, either due to their optimism or to the fury with which he defended the social demands of the left. From time to time even I am tempted to criticize him, and have done so, inside my head, many times. Once, however, in one of his books, I found a quote from Bertolt Brecht that he had underlined several times, an extract that explains a few things and taught me to read these articles of his with the perspective of the time: 'For we went, changing our country more often than our shoes. / In the class war, despairing / when there was only injustice and no resistance. / For we knew only too well: / Even the hatred of squalor / Makes the brow grow stern. / Even anger against injustice / Makes the voice grow harsh. Alas, we / Who wished to lay the foundations of kindness / Could not ourselves be kind. / But you, when at last it comes to pass / That man can help his fellow man, / Do not judge us / Too harshly.'

As I read through his articles from those years, nearly all of them published in Medellín's *El Mundo* newspaper, and a few in the Bogotá paper *El Tiempo*, some of his causes seem desperate. There is one particularly difficult, courageous article condemning torture, published shortly after a friend and student of his was detained and tortured by the army in Medellín:

'Before the President of the Republic and his ministers of War and Justice, and before the attorney general, I accuse the "interrogators" from the Bomboná Battalion from the city of Medellín, of engaging in the physical and psychological torture of those detained by the Fourth Brigade.

'I accuse them of putting detainees into the middle of a room, blindfolded and tied up, on foot, for whole days and nights, subjected to physical and psychological treatments of the most extreme cruelty, without letting them sit down for even a minute, without letting them sleep, beating and kicking different parts of their body, insulting them, letting them hear the screams of the other detainees in neighbouring rooms, removing their blindfolds only to let them see how they pretend to rape their wives, how they load a gun with bullets and take the detainees out to go for a walk on the edge of the city threatening them with death if they don't confess and inform on their supposed "accomplices"; lying to them about so-called "confessions" from other torture victims, forcing them to kneel down and making them open their legs to impossibly extreme physical limits, to cause them incredibly intense pain, made worse by the interrogators standing on top of them, all the while carrying on the continuous, exhausting, intense "interrogation"; leaving the windows in their room open in the early hours of the morning and the shirtless detainees shivering with cold; allowing their lower limbs to develop dropsy due to being forced to remain upright and motionless, until the cramps, pain, and physical and mental despair become unbearable, leading some to throw themselves out of the windows, to slit their wrists with pieces of glass, to scream and cry like children or madmen, or to tell fantastic, imaginary stories, whatever it takes to escape a little from the extreme ordeal imposed on them.

'I accuse the interrogators of the Bombona Battalion of Medellín of being merciless torturers with no soul and no compassion for human beings, of being trained psychopaths, of being criminals on the government payroll, paid for by Colombians to reduce political and trade union detainees of all categories to conditions incompatible with human dignity, of causing all kind of trauma, frequently irreversible and irremediable, with life-long consequences.

'I formally and publicly denounce these procedures of the so-called *middle managers*, which systematically violate the human rights of hundreds of our fellow countrymen.

'And I accuse any among the highest command of the army and the nation who read this article, of criminal complicity, if they do not immediately put a stop to this situation that offends the most basic feelings of human solidarity of those Colombians not suffering from insanity or fanaticism.'

Brave, clear denunciations like this provoked anger in the army and among some government officials, but not answers. Very occasionally a judge or an attorney would attempt to register his accusations. But in general they were answered with nothing but a hostile silence. And the hostility increased year by year until the denouement. Once my sister Vicky, who moved in the highest and richest circles of the city, said to my father: 'Daddy, people don't love you in Medellín.' And he answered, 'Darling, there are lots of people who love me, but you won't find them in your circle of friends, they're in a different place, and one day I'll take you to meet them.' Vicky says that on the day of the procession that accompanied my father's funeral through the centre of town, with thousands of people waving white handkerchiefs as they marched, and from windows, and in the cemetery, she suddenly understood at that moment that my father was taking her to meet the people who loved him.

It would take a very long time to transcribe all the

articles in which my father denounced, often with first and last names, the violations committed by state officials or members of the police against defenceless citizens. He did it for years, though sometimes this struggle seemed to him like nothing but a cry in the desert. The eviction of indigenous people from landowners' haciendas (along with the murder of the priest who was supporting their cause); the disappearance of a student; the torture of a professor; protests bloodily repressed; the murders repeated every year like a macabre ritual of trade union leaders; the unjustifiable kidnappings by the guerrilla fighters ... He denounced all these things time and time again, amid the silent fury of his targets, who chose to ignore his words in the hope that they would disappear into oblivion through a strategy of silence or indifference.

Where he was most radical was in his search for a more just society, less despicable than classist, discriminatory Colombian society. He didn't preach violent revolution, but he did advocate a radical change in the State's priorities, warning that if all citizens were not at least given equal opportunities, as well as the minimal conditions for decent survival, as soon as possible, we would be bound to suffer for a long time to come from violence, delinquency, the emergence of armed gangs and furious guerrilla groups.

'A human society that aspires to be *just* must provide the same opportunities in terms of the physical, cultural and social environment to every one of its members. If it does not do this, it will create artificial inequalities. The physical, cultural and social environment into which a rich child and a poor child are born, for example, are very different in Colombia. The first are born in clean houses, with good facilities, with book-lined studies, with games and music. The second are born in slums, or in houses without bathrooms, in neighbourhoods without playgrounds, schools or medical services. The first attend luxurious private clinics, the second oversubscribed health centres. The first go to excellent schools. The second to wretched ones. Are we giving them the same opportunities? Quite the contrary. From the moment they are born they are placed in unequal, unjust conditions. Even before they are born, they start their intrauterine lives in inferior conditions, because of the food their mothers consume. In the San Vicente Hospital we have weighed and measured groups of children who were born in the Private Wing (for families who are able to pay for medical treatment) and those born in the so-called Charity Wing (families who are able to pay very little or nothing at all for these services) and we have found that the average weight and height at birth is much greater (by a statistically significant degree) among those born in the private section than those in the charity section. Which means that they are *born unequal*. And not due to biological factors, but to social factors (the living conditions, unemployment and hunger of their parents).

'These are irrefutable and evident truths that no one can deny. Why then do we deny them, striving to maintain such a situation? Because egotism and indifference make people blind to evidence and make those who are satisfied with their own good living conditions deny the bad conditions others live in. They do not want to see what is in full view, so that they can preserve the privileged situation they enjoy. What can be done about this state of affairs? Who is responsible for taking action? It is obvious that those who must act are the ones negatively affected. But almost always, in the midst of their needs, worries and tragedies, they are not conscious of this objective situation, they do not take it in, they do not make it subjective.

'It may seem paradoxical, but it has ever been thus: it is some of those whom life has placed in acceptable conditions who have had to raise the awareness of the oppressed and exploited in order that they react and work to change the unjust circumstances affecting them unfavourably. This is how important changes have been brought about in the living conditions of many countries' inhabitants and there is no doubt that we are living through a period of history in which groups of people—ethically superior to us—do not accept as *natural* the fact that these situations of inequality and injustice should go on. Their fight against the "establishment" is a hard and dangerous fight. They must confront the anger and unease of the most powerful political and economic groups. They must face the consequences, even those incompatible with their own peace and possibilities; incompatible with attaining so-called "success" in established society.

'But there is an inner force that impels them to work in favour of those who need their help. For many of them, this force has become their reason for living. This struggle gives meaning to their lives. Living is justified if the world is a little better when one dies, as a result of one's work and efforts. To live simply for pleasure is a legitimate animal ambition. But for human beings, for *Homo sapiens*, it is to be content with very little. In order to distinguish ourselves from other animals, in order to justify our time on this earth, we must aspire to goals superior to the mere enjoyment of life. *The fixation on goals distinguishes some men from others.* And here the most important thing is not to achieve those goals, but to fight for them. We cannot all be the protagonists of history. We are all merely cells in the universal human body, but we should be aware that each of us can do something to improve the world in which we live and in which those who come after us will live. We must work for the present and for the future, and this will bring us more happiness than simple pleasure in material goods. The knowledge that we are contributing to building a better world, must be the highest of human aspirations.'

In everything he wrote one can feel his strong humanist, emotional, vibrant tone. He used his authoritative, convincing voice to try and get all people, rich and poor, to wake up and strive to do something to improve the iniquitous conditions in the country. He did so until the last day of his life, in a desperate attempt to combat with words the barbaric actions of a state that was and is unwilling to do anything other than maintain the great injustices that exist, and defends this intolerable injustice however it can, even down to the murder of those who wish to change it.

36

I don't want to write hagiography and I'm not interested in portraying a man without any of the weaknesses of human nature. If my father had been a little less vain, if he could have relinquished his desire to stand out, if he'd sometimes reined in his passion for justice, which occasionally turned into an avenging fanaticism, especially towards the end of his life, perhaps he would have been more efficient. He lacked the determination and perseverance needed to complete the excess of projects he undertook. He himself recognized this defect and often said: 'I'm a very good father, but a very bad mother,' by which he meant he was good at fertilizing, at planting the seed of a good idea, but did not have the patience for gestation and nurturing.

He did stupid things, as we all do. He got involved with absurd movements; his ingenuousness meant that he was often deceived; and he sometimes served as a spokesman for the interests of people who knew how to manipulate him through flattery. When he realized he'd been used, he always repeated the same comical and disappointed phrase: 'All my intelligence has ever done for me is make me stupid.' He was ashamed, for example, of having sectioned my sister Maryluz's brother-in-law, who was overwrought one night and said he was being pursued by mafiosos. My father could not imagine that there could be mafiosos in Medellín in the 1970s. Much less what this young man, Jota Vélez, was saying, when he repeated like a madman that these gangsters were killing people, threatening others, exporting cocaine and marijuana, buying women in the poor neighbourhoods, paying hit men and thugs ... My father mistook these truths for the ravings of a lunatic, for schizophrenia, and they took Jota, in a straitjacket, to the Bello psychiatric hospital. When everything that Jota said started to come true, and his monstrous fears began to be realized day in and day out in a city descending into barbarity, my father was forced to admit that he himself had been mad with blindness and naïveté, and to apologize to Jota, whose impassioned and lucid denunciations he had rejected as demented delirium.

He also joined a friendship committee between the peoples of Colombia and North Korea, because they knew how to flatter his vanity. He even brought home books by Kim Il-sung, on the 'Juche idea,' and participated in an embarrassing congress in Portugal devoted to analysing the thought of this megalomaniacal and bloodthirsty twentieth-century dictator. The worst of it was that my father realized it was nonsense—when he spoke of the Juche idea he would laugh in derision and bafflement—but the fact was that he had joined this group. Who knows why he let himself be carried along by the current, why he was unable to avoid this dishonourable complicity with a dictatorship. He never wanted to go to North Korea, perhaps sensing that he would no longer be able to maintain such falsehood if he were to see first-hand the distance between the words and the reality.

On occasion, during the last years of his life, he was manipulated by the extreme left in Colombia. Although he detested the armed struggle, he did try to understand and almost excuse (though never explicitly) the insurgents and the guerrillas; and since he agreed with some of their ideological positions (agrarian and urban reform, redistribution of wealth, hatred of monopolies, loathing of an oligarchic and corrupt class that had brought the most shameful poverty and inequality to the country), he sometimes looked the other way when it was the guerrillas committing atrocities: attacks on barracks, absurd explosions. But he always abhorred kidnappings and indiscriminate terrorist attacks against innocent victims. As is sometimes the case with human rights activists, he paid more attention to atrocities committed by the government than to those committed by the armed enemies of the government. He explained it in a more or less coherent way. It was more serious when a priest raped a child than when a pervert did; the guerrillas had declared themselves outside the law, but the government claimed to respect the law. This was true, but by that route one can easily lose one's way, and he sometimes lost it. This can never justify his murder, but can explain in part the murderous rage of those who killed him.

I remember we once argued about a (disputed) Pancho Villa quote, which he liked to repeat: 'Without justice there can be no peace.' Or even: 'Without justice there cannot—should not—be peace.' I asked him if the armed struggle was therefore necessary to combat injustice.

He replied that it had been necessary against Hitler; he wasn't a fanatical pacifist, but in the case of Colombia, he was absolutely sure the armed struggle was not the way, and that the existing conditions did not justify the guerrillas' use and abuse of force. He had faith that the country could be transformed through radical reforms. Never, not even when he was most furious at the atrocities committed by the army and the government, did his rage draw him out of his deep-rooted pacifism, and although he understood the route others, such as Camilo Torres and José Alvear Restrepo, had chosen, he didn't think it was the way out. He would have been quite incapable of pointing a rifle at anyone, or killing anyone, for any cause, or supporting with his words those who were using weapons. He preferred Gandhi's method: pacifist resistance even to the point of supreme sacrifice.

OPENING THE DRAWERS

37

One of the hardest things we have to do when someone dies, or is killed, is emptying and going through their drawers. Two weeks after his murder, I was assigned the task of going through my father's filing cabinets and desk drawers in his office (files, papers, correspondence, accounts). Maryluz and my mother would take charge of the ones at home. Opening drawers is like opening crevices into someone else's mind: what he was most fond of, who he had seen (according to his appointment book or notebook jottings), what he had eaten or purchased (receipts from department stores, credit card bills, invoices), what photos or souvenirs he treasured, which documents he kept on display and which ones in secret.

Something strange that happened was that Isabelita, who had been my father's secretary for the last ten years, had disappeared ever since the day of his death. Not in the tragic Latin American sense of the word: we knew she was fine. But she made it clear that she didn't want to see us, didn't want to return to the office, refused to answer anything anyone might want to ask her (either the family or the magistrates) and, in short, she was scared. It has been almost twenty years since anyone in my family has seen Isabelita, and by now I don't think any of us want to ask her anything. All the questions we so urgently needed to ask twenty years ago are now hidden away, or resolved in a personal and secret way, in the deepest part of our thoughts.

Some ten days after the crime I had to go to the morgue to collect my father's clothes and belongings. They handed them to me in a plastic bag and I took them to his office on Carrera Chile. I laid everything out on the patio: the bloodstained suit, the bullet-torn shirt, stained with blood, his tie, his shoes. Something fell out from the collar of his jacket and bounced hard against the ground. I looked closely: it was a bullet. The magistrates had not even taken the trouble to inspect his clothing. The next day I took this bullet to the police court, although I knew it would be of no use. The clothes smelled bad, so I burned them all, except for his shirt, which I left out in the sun to dry, with its terrible dark blood stains.

For many years, I secretly kept this bloodstained shirt, with lumps that turned brown and black with time. I don't know why I kept it. It was as if I wanted to have it there to goad me, to keep me from forgetting whenever my conscience grew numb, like a spur to memory, like a promise to avenge his death. When I wrote this book I burned it too, since I understood that the only revenge, the only memento, and also the only possibility to forget and to forgive, consisted in telling what happened, and nothing more.

During those days when I went through all his papers I gradually selected some fragments of his new and old writings, and put together a little book, which we later published with the help of the governor, Fernando Panesso Serna, who behaved very well towards my whole family from the first day, and the Minister of Education, a doctor, Antonio Yepes Parra, who had been a student of my father's and wanted to support this compilation that I later titled *Manual of Tolerance*. Carlos Gaviria wrote a prologue, which he sent us from his exile in Argentina.

Among the papers and documents that I went through in his office, I also found much more personal information, which I liked, although some of it also surprised me. My father had often told me that every human being, everyone's personality, is like a cube placed on top of a table. There's one face that we can all see (the top one); faces that some can see and others can't, which if we make an effort we can also see ourselves (the ones on the sides); and one face hidden from everyone, both from others and from ourselves (the face the cube is resting on). Opening a dead person's drawer is like examining that face that was only visible to him and that he wanted no one else to see, the face he protected from others: his private life.

My father had dropped many indirect hints about his private life. Not straight confessions, which tend to be as much of a burden to children as a relief to parents, but small hints and signs that let rays of light into his shadowy regions, into the interior of the cube that is the hidden container of our conscience. Those hints occupied a region inside me somewhere between knowledge and darkness, like those feelings we call intuition, but which we can't or don't want to confirm with facts, and don't allow to rise to the surface of our conscience in well-defined words, examples, experiences or irrefutable proofs.

Twice, for example, my father took me to see a film, Luchino Visconti's *Death in Venice*, that beautiful film based on Thomas Mann's short novel, in which a man in his declining years (Mann's model may have been Mahler, whose music is also used in the film, one of the director's wisest moves) feels excited by and succumbs to the absolute beauty represented by the figure of a Polish youth, Tadzio. Mann says that he did not want to have a girl symbolizing beauty, but rather a young man, so readers wouldn't think the admiration was purely sexual, a simple physical attraction. What the protagonist, Gustav von Aschenbach, felt, was something more, and also something less: an infatuation with an almost abstract body, the personification of a platonic ideal, symbolized by the androgynous beauty of an adolescent. I was too involved with my own world when my father insisted we go back to see the film for a third time, perhaps aware that I'd been unable to perceive its deepest and most hidden meaning.

A letter he wrote me in 1975, and published as an epilogue to his second book (*Letters from Asia*), contains the following reflections: 'For me, it has gradually become ever clearer that what I most admire is beauty. No matter that I've tried to be a scientist—though without quite succeeding—all my life. Or indeed to be a politician, which I would also have liked. It's possible that I might have been able to become a writer had I put my mind to it. But you are already beginning to understand and feel all the effort, work, anguish, isolation, solitude and intense pain that life demands of those who choose the difficult path of creating beauty. I'm sure you'll accept my invitation to go and see Visconti's *Death in Venice* together this evening. The first time I saw it I was impressed only by its form. The last time I understood its essence, its depths. We'll talk about it tonight.'

We went to see it again, that evening, but we didn't talk about it that night, perhaps because there was something I didn't want to understand at seventeen. I think only a decade later, after his death, and as I dug through his drawers did I really come to understand what my father had wanted me to see when he took me see *Death in Venice* again.

There are shadowy areas in all our lives. They are not necessarily shameful, and may even be the parts of our stories we're most proud of, those that in the end make us think, in spite of everything, that our time spent on this earth is justified. But they form part of our most intimate, private experience, and we prefer not to share them with anybody. Sometimes we may hide them away because we know that society would reject them as hateful or monstrous or dirty, although to us they are none of those things. And sometimes we conceal them because in truth, irrespective of the relative judgements of the time and culture in which we live, they are universally reprehensible, detestable facts, which human morals cannot abide.

I found no shadows of this last kind in my father's desk drawers, and what I did find makes him, in my eyes, even greater, more admirable and more valuable. But I respect his right to conceal these truths about himself, so I too will leave this drawer closed. To open it would do nothing but feed useless gossip worthy only of soap operas, and unworthy of a person who loved all the manifestations of human beauty and who was, at the same time, spontaneous and discreet.

38

There is a trivial and undoubted truth, which is nevertheless important always to keep in mind: we are all
going to die. The end result of all lives is the same. The
presence and awareness of death is one of the most strik-
ing features of classic Spanish lyric poetry. Some of the
best passages of literature speak of it with a beauty at
once stark and moving, with that paradoxical solace the
evocation of death has when dressed in the perfection
of art: St. John of the Cross, Cervantes, Quevedo ... My
father used to recite from memory some of Don Jorge
Manrique's *Couplets on the Death of his Father* so often on
our long walks through the countryside, that I ended
up learning them by heart as well, and I think they'll
accompany me, as they accompanied him, all my life,
their marvellous rhythm pounding in my skull, with
their perfect consoling melody that floats into our ears
and thoughts from the deepest folds of a conscience trying to explain the inexplicable:

O let the soul her slumbers break
Let thought be quickened, and awake:
Awake to see
How soon this life is past and gone,
And death comes softly stealing on,
How silently!

Swiftly our pleasures glide away,
Our hearts recall the distant day
With many sighs;
The moments that are speeding fast
We heed not, but the past—the past,
More highly prize.

Onward its course the present keeps,
Onward its course the current sweeps,
Till life is done;
And, did we judge of time aright,
The past and future in their flight
Would be as one.

Let no one fondly dream again,
That Hope in all her shadowy train
Will not decay;
Fleeting as were the dreams of old,
Remembered like a tale that's told,
They pass away.

Our lives are rivers, gliding free
To that unfathomed, boundless sea,
The silent grave!
Thither all earthly pomp and boast
Roll, to be swallowed up and lost
In one dark wave ...

Thither the mighty torrents stray
Thither the brook pursues its way,
And tinkling rill.
There all are equal; side by side
The poor man and the son of pride
Lie calm and still.

We know we're going to die, simply by virtue of being alive. We know the what (that we'll die), but not the when, or the how, or the where. And although the ending is certain, inevitable, when what always comes to pass happens to another, we like to find out the very moment, and recount the intricacies of the how, and know the details of the where and conjecture about the why. Of all possible deaths there is one we can accept with resignation: dying of old age, in one's own bed, after a full, intense and useful life. 'Maestro Don Rodrigo Manrique, so famous and so valiant' died like that, and so those couplets by his son, Don Jorge, although they tell of his father's death, have not just a resigned but, in a certain sense, a happy ending. The father does not only accept his own death, but receives it with pleasure:

As thus the dying warrior prayed,
Without one gathering mist or shade
Upon his mind;
Encircled by his family,
Watched by affection's gentle eye
So soft and kind;

His soul to Him, who gave it, rose;
God lead it to its long repose,
Its glorious rest!
And, though the warrior's sun has set,

Its light shall linger round us yet,
Bright, radiant, blest.

Elderly, peacefully aware and surrounded by loved ones. That is the only death we can serenely accept and remember with consolation. Almost all other deaths are odious, and the most unacceptable and absurd is that of a child or a young person, or the death caused by the murderous violence of another human being. Consciousness rebels at these, and the pain and rage, at least in my case, does not ease. I have never resigned myself to my sister's death, nor have I ever been able calmly to accept my father's murder. It is true that, in a way, he was satisfied with his life, and ready to die if necessary, but he despised the violent kind of death that was being planned for him. It is this that is most painful and most unacceptable. This book is an attempt to leave a record of that pain, a record at once useless and necessary. Useless because time does not run backwards and events do not change, but necessary at least for me, because my life and work would lack meaning if I did not write what I feel I have to write, and that in almost twenty years of trying have never been able to write, until now.

On Monday 24 August 1987, very early, around six-thirty in the morning, a radio station telephoned my father to tell him that his name was on a list of people who were being threatened in Medellín, people who, it said, would be killed. They read him the relevant paragraph: 'Héctor Abad Gómez: President of the Antioquia Human Rights Defence Committee. Medic to guerrillas, false democrat, dangerous due to popular sympathy in upcoming Medellín mayoral elections. Useful idiot of the Communist Party.' They interviewed my father on air and he asked them to read out some of the other names on the list. They did so. Among them were the journalist Jorge Child, the former Minister of Foreign Relations Alfredo Vásquez Carrizosa, the columnist Alberto Aguirre, the political leader Jaime Pardo Leal (assassinated a few months later), the writer Patricia Lara, the lawyer Eduardo Umaña Luna, the singer Carlos Vives, and many others. The only thing my father said was that he felt very honoured to be in the company of such fine and important people, who did so many good things for the country. After the interview, off the air, he asked the journalist to send a photocopy of the list to his office.

Ten days earlier, on 14 August, the left-wing senator, Pedro Luis Valencia had been killed. He was also a doctor and a professor at the university, and my father organized and led a march 'for the right to life' on the 19th in protest at his murder. This huge march passed through the streets of Medellín in silence, culminating in Berrío Park, where my father gave the only speech. Many people saw it on television, or saw it pass by from the windows of their offices, and later told us what they'd thought: they'll kill him too; they're going to kill him. His penultimate article was about that crime, a denunciation of the paramilitaries. He also gave a lecture in the Pontificia Bolivariana University where he accused the army and government officials of complicity with the criminals.

That same Monday 24 August, at midday, he telephoned Alberto Aguirre at home (having been trying him all morning at his office) and convinced him to request a meeting with the mayor, William Jaramillo, to find out a little about the source of the threats, and maybe to ask for some protection; they arranged to meet on the Wednesday at eleven, in my father's office. On the afternoon of the same day, the Human Rights Committee of Antioquia met and, given the gravity of the situation, decided to draft a press release denouncing the death squads and paramilitary groups that were operating in the city and killing people linked to the university. Present at this meeting, among others, were Carlos Gaviria, Leonardo Betancur and Carlos Gónima. Leonardo and my father were murdered the next day; Carlos Gónima, a few months later, on 22 February; Carlos Gaviria escaped with his life by fleeing the country.

At the end of this meeting, Carlos Gaviria asked my father how seriously he was taking the personal threat that he'd spoken of on the radio. My father invited him to stay and talk for a while so he could tell him. He opened a small bottle of whisky in the shape of a bell (which Carlos took away empty and still keeps in his study as a memento), read him the list they'd sent him, and, while he acknowledged that the threat was serious, repeated that he felt very proud to be in such fine company: 'I don't want to be killed, far from it, but maybe it wouldn't be the worst of deaths; and if they do kill me, it might serve some purpose.' Carlos went home feeling distressed.

Several times, during those days, my father spoke of death in an ambiguous tone that seemed somewhere between resignation and fear. He had reflected a lot, and over a long period, on his own death. One of the few short stories he ever wrote dealt with this theme, with death's mythical figure, an old woman dressed in black with a scythe over her shoulder, who visits him once, but grants him a stay of execution. Among the papers I organized after his death, and published under the title *Manual of Tolerance*, I found this reflection: 'Montaigne said that philosophy was useful because it taught us how to die. For me, closer to the last stage than the first in this birth-to-death process we call life, the subject of death is becoming ever simpler, more natural and I'd even say—not as a subject but as a reality—more desirable. And it's not that I am disillusioned with anything or anybody. Maybe just the opposite. Because I think I have lived fully, intensely, sufficiently.'

He was undoubtedly prepared to die, but this does not mean he wanted to be killed. In an interview he'd given that same week, he was asked about death or, rather, about the possibility that he would be killed, and he answered: 'I am very satisfied with my life and I don't fear death, but I still have many joys: being with my grandchildren, tending to my roses and conversing with my wife. Yes, while I do not fear death, I don't want to be killed either: I want to die surrounded by my children and grandchildren, calmly [...] A violent death must be terrifying, I wouldn't like it at all.'

39

That Tuesday 25 August my eldest sister and I got up at dawn to go to La Inés, the farm south east of Medellín by the River Cauca that my father had inherited from Grandpa Antonio. We were having a pool put in and it was due to be finished that day. Since there was no road to the house, we'd asked our neighbour Doña Lucía de la Cuesta for permission to let the workers bring the iron posts and building materials for the pool across the pastures of her farm, Kalamarí. The Suzuki Jeep loaded with cement and stones had made so many trips that a little path had formed across the field, and Maryluz and I went along there to meet the work crew. For the first time we saw the pool filled with water, and we felt happy in anticipation of all the enjoyment it would give us. We were back in Medellín before noon. My sister had brought my father two big passion fruits as a gift: they were the first from a vine he'd planted in the garden a few months earlier.

Maryluz wanted to give him a surprise in December,

when we planned to spend the holidays at the farm, so she didn't want to tell him over lunch that day where they'd built the pool—whether behind or in front of the house—and she told him a little white lie as well to add to the surprise: that there hadn't been enough money to knock down a low wall my father didn't like that enclosed a narrow porch. Doña Lucía de la Cuesta phoned around noon, to tell my father that since the pool was now completed, she was withdrawing the permission to drive across her land, since if we carried on doing so, it would turn into a right of way. My father asked her if she wouldn't even let him drive in by himself in December and Lucía said, in a friendly tone, no, he was quite fit and could get there on horseback. 'And what about when I'm old and can't get ride anymore?' my father persisted, and Lucía said: 'That's a long way off, Héctor. We'll see when the time comes.' Doña Lucía herself told me this conversation word for word, years later; everyone who spoke to him that day has a clear and precise memory of it.

At that time my father was in the running for Liberal Party mayoral candidate; that year would be the first time in Colombia that mayors would be directly elected, and on the Thursday my father had arranged a luncheon meeting at the Rionegro farm with Dr. Germán Zea Hernández, who was coming from Bogotá to try to get the Liberal candidates to agree to back a single name. Bernardo Guerra, president of the Liberal Directorate, was opposed to my father's nomination, though he had the best chance of winning, and had even refused to attend the Thursday lunch at the farm. My mother had been cooking and making preparations for that lunch since Tuesday. Another of my sisters, Vicky, was preparing to host a meal at her house on the Friday; the dissident Liberal leaders would all attend, among them her former boyfriend, Álvaro Uribe Vélez, then a senator. In spite of his personal naïveté in political matters, my father had good intuition about people who might be able to rise to the top. In the last interview he gave, and which was published posthumously in *El Espectador* in November 1987, he declared the following: 'At this moment I like Ernesto Samper Pizano and Álvaro Uribe Vélez; they have good proposals.' Years later both would become president of Colombia.

That same Tuesday, the morning of the 25th, Luis Felipe Vélez, head of the Antioquia teachers' guild, was murdered on the doorstep of the union headquarters. My father was outraged. Many years later, in a book published in 2001, Carlos Castaño, ringleader of the paramilitaries for more than ten years, would confess how the group he led in Medellín, in consultation with Army intelligence, assassinated, among many other victims, Senator Pedro Luis Valencia, in front of his small children, as well as the leader of the teachers' union, Luis Felipe Vélez. They accused both of being kidnappers.

At midday on that Tuesday, as they drove home for lunch together, my mother told us later how my father had been trying to get news about the Luis Felipe Vélez crime, but that every station had nothing on but football. For my father the excess of sports news was the new opiate of the masses, what kept them numb, unaware of what was really going on, and he'd written about this on several occasions. In the car with my mother, he had punched the steering wheel and said angrily: 'The city's going to ruin, but they won't talk about anything except football.' My mother says that he was shaken that day, with a mixture of rage and sadness, almost on the verge of despair.

That same morning, 25 August, my father had spent

some time at the Faculty of Medicine, and then in his office on the second floor of the building where my mother had her business on Carrera Chile, next door to the house Alberto Aguirre had grown up in and where his brother still lived. It was now the headquarters of the Human Rights Committee of Antioquia. I suppose it must have been at some point during that morning when my father copied out by hand the Borges sonnet he had in his pocket when they killed him, along with the death list. The poem is called 'Epitaph' and goes like this:

Already we are the oblivion we shall be—
the elemental dust that does not know us,
the dust that once was red Adam and now is
all men, the dust we shall not see.
Already we are the two dates on the headstone,
the beginning and the end. The coffin,
the obscene decay and the shroud,
the death rites and the dirges.
I am not some fool who clings
to the magical sound of his own name.
I think, with hope, of that man
who will never know I walked the earth.
Beneath the blue indifference of heaven,
I find this thought consoling.

In the afternoon he went back to his office, wrote his column for the newspaper, had a few meetings with his campaign staff and arranged to meet the publicity people at the Liberal Directorate in the evening. That night they were planning to plaster the city with posters with the name and picture of the candidate. Before going to the Directorate, a woman whose name we do not know and who we've never seen since, suggested to my father that he go to the teachers' union to pay his last respects to their murdered leader. My father thought it a good idea, and even invited Carlos Gaviria and Leonardo Betancur to come with him, and that's where he was going when I saw him for the last time.

We bumped into each other at the entrance to the office. I was arriving with my mother, driving her car, and he was coming out of the door accompanied by a heavy-set woman in a purple dress, who looked like the sorrowful statues in Holy Week processions. When I saw them, I teased my mother: 'Look, Mum, there's Dad cheating on you with another woman.' My father came over to the car and we got out. Beaming, as always, when he saw me, he planted his loudest kiss on my cheek and asked me how my meeting at the university had gone.

I had returned from Italy a few months earlier, 28 years old, with a companion, a daughter who was just starting to walk, and no job. To get by I was writing letters and circulars, taking minutes and managing buildings for my mother's business until something more relevant to what I'd studied came along. My father had arranged for me to meet that afternoon with a key professor in the Humanities Department, Víctor Álvarez, and I had just had an interview with him. It had been a disappointing meeting, and the professor had given me no grounds for hope regarding the next applications for part-time teaching posts. My degree wasn't recognized by the University of Antioquia, and furthermore, all the positions in modern literature were completely full. We'd have to see in the future, maybe next year. I told my father the outcome of my interview and saw the deep disappointment on his face. He had immeasurable confidence in me and thought that everyone should receive me with open arms and all doors should be wide open for me. His face darkened for a second, with a mixture of sadness and surprise at my failure, then suddenly his face brightened again as if a good thought had crossed his mind at the same time, and with a happy smile, he said the last thing he'd say to me in his life (ten minutes later he'd be killed), along with the usual goodbye kiss:

'Don't worry, my love. You'll see, one day they'll be the ones calling you.'

That's what he was saying when his dearest student, Leonardo Betancur, arrived on his motorcycle. My father greeted him effusively, made him go up to his office to sign the Human Rights Committee's latest statement (they'd drafted it the night before and now had a clean copy), and invited him to come with him for a moment to the murdered teacher's wake, three blocks away, at the union headquarters. They walked off, in conversation, and my mother and I went inside the office, I to prepare for a board meeting, which was at six, and she to her own work. It was about quarter past five in the afternoon.

40

What happened afterwards I didn't see, but I can reconstruct it from what various witnesses told me, or from what I read in File number 319 of the Criminal Court of First Instance, for the crime of homicide and personal injury, opened 26 August 1987, and archived a few years later, without any arrests or suspects, without any clarification, without any result whatsoever. This investigation, read now, almost twenty years later, seems more like a textbook cover-up and conspiracy for impunity than a serious investigation. A month after the case was opened the judge in charge was sent on vacation, and officials from Bogotá were put in charge of keeping a close watch on the investigation, that is, to prevent any serious investigating.

My father, Leonardo and the woman walked down Carrera Chile to Calle Argentina and turned left there, walking up the street on the north sidewalk. They arrived at the corner of El Palo and crossed the street. They carried on up to Girardot. They passed Girardot and at the next corner knocked on the door of Adida (*Asociación de Institutores de Antioquia*), the teachers' union. Someone opened the door and a little crowd formed as other teachers were arriving at the same time, to find out what was going on. They had taken Luis Felipe Vélez's body to a funeral home more than two hours earlier and were having a protest demonstration at the Coliseo. My father was taken aback and looked around for the woman who'd accompanied him there, but she was no longer at his side; she had disappeared.

One of the witnesses says a motorbike with two young men on it came up Calle Argentina, slowly at first, then very quickly. They looked like they'd just come from the barber's, says someone else, with the closely cropped hair typical of soldiers and some hit men. They stopped the bike in front of the union building, left it running beside the curb, and both of them headed towards the little group in front of the door, pulling guns out of the waistband of their trousers.

Did my father see them, did he know they were about to kill him? For almost twenty years I have tried to be him there, facing death, at that moment. I imagine myself at sixty-five years of age, dressed in a suit and tie, asking at the door of a union about the wake of a leader murdered that morning. He would have asked about the crime of a few hours earlier, and they would have just told him that Luis Felipe Vélez had been killed there, right where he was standing. My father looks down at the ground, at his feet, as if he wanted to see the murdered teacher's blood. He doesn't see a trace of anything, but he hears quick footsteps coming towards him, and a hurried breathing that seems to pant down his neck. He looks up and sees the malevolent face of the assassin, sees the flashes coming out of the barrel of the pistol, hears at the same time the shots and feels the blow to his chest that knocks him down. He falls on his back, his glasses fly off and break, and on the ground, while he thinks for the last time, I'm sure, of all those he loves, his side racked with pain, he catches a confused glimpse of the mouth of the revolver that spits fire again and finishes him off with several shots to the head, the neck, and the chest again. Six shots, which means one of the hit men emptied his magazine. Meanwhile the other thug chases Leonardo Betancur inside the union building and kills him there. My father does not see his beloved student die; he doesn't actually see anything anymore, doesn't remember anything anymore; he bleeds, and in a very few moments his heart stops and his mind goes out.

He is dead and I don't know. He is dead and my mother doesn't know, my sisters don't know, his friends don't know, he himself doesn't know. I am at the meeting, which is just starting. The chair of the board, the lawyer and graphologist Alberto Posada Ángel (who will be stabbed to death a few years later), reads the minutes of the previous meeting, and another man arrives a little late and, before sitting down, tells us that he just saw someone killed a few blocks from there. He describes the hit man's bullets, says how horrible Medellín has become. Almost carelessly, I ask who the dead man could be. He does not know. At that moment I'm called to the phone. It's odd to be interrupted mid-meeting, but they say it's urgent, and I go out. It is a journalist, an old acquaintance of mine, who says: 'Just wanted to hear your voice, they're saying here that you've been killed.' I say no, I'm fine, and hang up, but in that very instant I think again and realize who the dead man is, without being told. If someone is saying Héctor Abad was killed it's because someone with my name has been killed. I go straight to my mother's office and say: 'I think the worst has happened.'

My mother is on the phone talking to her friend Gloria Villegas de Molina. She hangs up quickly and asks me: 'Héctor's been killed?' I tell her I think so. We stand up, we want to go to the place where they say there's a dead person. We ask the man in the board meeting and he gives us hope. 'No, no, I know the doctor and it wasn't him.' We go anyway. A messenger from the office goes ahead. We walk the same route my father and Leonardo took minutes before: Carrera Chile, left on Argentina, across El Palo. As we approach Girardot, we see from the distance a crowd of onlookers gathered around the door of a building, the union headquarters. The messenger emerges from the small group and nods affirmatively: 'Yes, it is the doctor, it's him.' We run and there he is, face up, in a pool of blood, under a sheet with a growing, dense, dark red stain. I know I take his hand and kiss him on the cheek, his cheek that is still warm. I know I scream and cry out insults, and that my mother throws herself down and embraces him. I don't know how much later I see my sister Clara arrive with Alfonso, her husband. Then Carlos Gaviria arrives, with his face contorted in pain and I shout at him to go away, to hide, that he has to go because we don't want any more deaths. My sister, my brother-in-law, my mother and I surround the body. My mother takes off his wedding ring and I take the papers out of his pockets. Later I'll see what they are: the photocopied hit list, and the poem, Borges' epitaph copied out in my father's handwriting, splashed with blood: 'Already we are the oblivion we shall be.'

At this moment I cannot cry. I feel a dry, tearless sadness. A complete sadness, but dumbfounded, incredulous.

Now that I'm writing it I am able to cry, but at that moment I was overcome by a sense of stupor. An almost serene astonishment at the scale of the evil, a rage without rage, a tearless weeping, a pain inside that doesn't seem moved but paralyzed, a quiet disquiet. I try to think, try to understand. I promise myself that all my life I will face the murderers calmly. I am on the verge of collapse, but I will not let myself collapse. Sons of bitches, I shout, it's all I shout, sons of bitches! And still inside, every day, I shout the same thing, what they are, what they were, what they still are if they're alive: sons of bitches!

While my mother and I are sitting next to my father's inert body, my sisters and our friends still don't know, but they gradually find out. The whole family, my four sisters, all my nephews and nieces, we each have a clear memory of the moment when we found out he'd been killed. One afternoon, at La Inés, looking out over the land and scenery my father left to us, we each took turns telling what we were doing and what happened to us that afternoon.

Maryluz, the eldest, told how she was in the living room of her house. She got a phone call from Néstor González, who had just heard the news on the radio, but he couldn't bring himself to tell her. He only asked, after much beating around the bush: 'And your father? How's your father?' 'Very well, busy with his campaign and human rights work as usual.' Néstor hung up, unable to tell her. Then another friend phoned, Alicia Gil, and she also couldn't give her the news, which she'd just heard on the radio. A moment later Maryluz saw a pair of men's shoes come in. Looking up she saw a briefcase. It was Mono Martínez. 'What miracle brings you here?' my sister asked him. 'Mary, something horrible's happened.'

And she knew: 'My dad's been killed?'

We all guessed, before we knew. 'After a first moment of madness,' Maryluz told us, 'I calmed down and I was very composed. I didn't cry; I reassured the others. Juan David (her eldest son, my parents' first grandchild and the one my father loved most) screamed and punched the walls, and ran down the street, from my house to Aba's house (the grandchildren all called their grandfather Aba). My friends arrived screaming. Martis got an excited phone call from a little girl in her class: "Hey, Martis, great news, there's no school tomorrow because they killed some really important man." Pili (her other daughter, who was six) locked herself in her room and wouldn't open the door to anybody: "I have a lot to study, I've got tons of homework, please don't interrupt me!" she shouted. Ricky was with his cousins, Clara's kids.'

Maryluz also told us how old grudges resurfaced at that moment. She told her friends: 'Tell Iván Saldarriaga not to even think of coming over here.' He was the owner of an ice cream factory and he and Maryluz, a long time ago, had had an argument about what my father said and wrote. She had said to him, at the end of the discussion: 'If they end up killing my father, don't even think of coming to the funeral.' When he arrived that evening, in tears, she forgave him. Saldarriaga paid for an announcement in the newspaper and bought food for everyone who came to the funeral.

Maryluz went on: 'Everyone asked me, at the wake, why I wasn't crying. I only cried when I saw Edilso, our dear caretaker from the Rionegro farm, arrive with an enormous bunch of roses that Dad had grown, and place them on top of the coffin. At that moment I couldn't take any more and burst into tears. I didn't cry at the burial. I saw my friends behind the trees in the Campos de Paz cemetery. I remember Fernán Ángel behind a tree, afraid there would be gunfire, a panic, something. It was a fearful funeral, with lots of people shouting slogans, and armed men prowling around the house and the cemetery. Many people thought they'd be killed, that a shootout or a riot would break out. I remember when Carlos Gaviria spoke, the papers in his hand trembled, but he spoke very well. Manuel Mejía Vallejo also gave a speech, with a megaphone, beside the grave.'

I still have Mejía Vallejo's and Carlos Gaviria's speeches. The former, a novelist, born in Jericó, the same village as my father, spoke of the imminent threat of oblivion: 'We live in a country that forgets its best faces, its best impulses, and so life will go on, irremediably monotonous, in forgetfulness of those who give us our raison d'être, our reasons to go on living. I know your absence will be mourned and real tears will fall from eyes that saw you and knew you. But then that terrible erasure will come, because we in this land so easily forget what we love most, as our lives sink into horror. And when that oblivion arrives, it will be like a monster that sweeps everything aside, and not even your name will be remembered. I know your death will be futile, and your heroism will become just one more absence.'

Carlos concentrated on the figure of the humanist confronting a deteriorating country: 'What did Héctor Abad do to deserve this fate? The answer has to be given as a sort of counterpoint, contrasting the things he embodied with the value system that now prevails among us. As befits his profession, he fought for life, and the killers won that battle; in keeping with his academic vocation and his way of life, he struggled against ignorance, recognizing it, in the Socratic tradition, as the source of all evil that oppresses the world. But the murderers addressed him with Millán Astray's barbarous expression: "Long live death, down with intelligence!" With the conscience of a just and civilized man he decided he would make the fight for the rule of law his priority, while those who were assigned this task within the State showed more faith in the banquet of shrapnel.'

Maryluz also remembers that the night of the 25th, although she didn't want to go to the crime scene, she went to my father's office, shortly after finding out what had happened. There we all gathered, except Sol, who locked herself in her room and wouldn't come out until very late. She remembers another detail: 'That morning, Héctor, on the way back from La Inés, near Santa Bárbara, you had said to me: "Except for Marta's death, we've been very lucky, with this beautiful place in the country, everyone in the family doing so well." And I'd answered that of course we had, because life rewards the good. We hadn't done anyone any harm, so why shouldn't things go well for us, I said. The first thing you shouted at me that night in our father's office, was that: "Oh yes, of course, we've never done anyone any harm so things are always going to go well for us, right? Look what's happened to my dad for being good to everybody." You were angry with the whole world. Later Alberto Aguirre's sister-in-law came in, Sonia Martínez, who lived next door and had been Marta's guitar teacher, and you shouted at her: "Tell Aguirre to get away from Colombia right now, he's next and we don't want any more deaths!"'

Clara, my second oldest sister, remembers she was in a meeting with Alfonso Arias, her husband, and Carlos López, in Ultra Advertising. They left there before six to go to the office. López knew within a few minutes and was thinking, please don't let them turn on the radio.

Clara and Alfonso didn't turn it on; they arrived at the office and as Clara tells it:

'As we arrived I saw a lot of people outside. At first I thought it was strange, and then I thought it might be normal as it was the end of the working day. When I stopped, I saw that everyone was looking at me strangely. Something was different. Ligia, who lived in an apartment in the office building, came slowly towards the car. I didn't dare get out, I was shaking, I thought something horrible must have happened from the way they were looking at me. Ligia came to the car window: "I have bad news. Your father's been killed." I asked to be taken to where he was, and no one wanted to take me. Darío Muñoz, the courier, said: "I'll take her." I was walking there with him and Alfonso. At that moment I felt something hot running down my legs. I had a terrible haemorrhage, just like the haemorrhage I had when Mum and Dad got on the plane with Marta when she was ill, to bring her home to Medellín. It was a dreadful haemorrhage. Gushing. I was desperate, while I was walking and running those few blocks from the office. I was like a madwoman. When we got close I saw the uproar, the crowd. "Over there?" I asked the messenger. "Yes, over there." When I got there Mamá and Quiquín were already there. I couldn't believe it, just couldn't believe it.

'I saw Vicky on a street corner. She was hanging back. I called her: "Vicky, come here, come here!" Why wasn't Vicky coming over? She kept walking back and forth around the corner, but she wouldn't come over, she couldn't. They tried to take the body away, but we wanted all his children to see him. We said, I don't know why: "We won't let them take him until Maryluz and Solbia arrive. If we have to we'll sit on top of him. They have to see what's been done to him." The judge arrived, and told us they had to take him, that a riot was going to break out. Alfonso convinced us and we finally let them take his body away. Several of them picked him up by the arms and legs, and threw him carelessly into the back of a pickup truck, they threw him violently, as if he were a sack of potatoes, with no respect, and that hurt me, as if they were breaking his bones, even though he wouldn't feel anything anymore.'

Alfonso Arias, Clara's husband at the time, remembers that when he arrived at the scene with my sister his blood pressure dropped and he thought he was going to faint. 'We were crouched down there, beside your father, and when I stood up the world went black and I almost keeled over, but no one noticed. It was after his death that I began to find out about all the recognition your father had received and how important he was to society, to the country, and to so many people. In daily life we just saw him as one of the family, a wonderful father and grandfather, but we didn't appreciate how great he was and all that he stood for, and the huge impact his death had, the amount of people he'd helped, without anyone in the family knowing about it. On weekends he used to read us the drafts of the articles he was going to publish in the newspaper the following week; we'd read and discuss them and give our opinions on them. It was something so normal for us, and we didn't realize the value of those articles. I valued him as a person and as a human being, but as a public figure with social impact I came to value him much more after his death.

'I devoted myself to looking after your father's roses in Rionegro very affectionately, with love really, for several years. I liked doing it because it was like a homage to him. The image of your dad in his straw hat and muddy blue jeans kneeling by his rose bushes is the loveliest image I have of him. That garden represented a lot, it was like a symbol and your father saw it that way too. It wasn't just a hobby, he was saying something by devoting so much time and so much work to beauty. Something that has no use, that's simply beautiful. Your father, by devoting so much effort and so much work to that, was saying something. There was an implicit message in it. I wanted to receive that message. I still pass by there and see it through the window sometimes, because when the planes come in to land they pass right over his rose bed, and I see fleeting glimpses of colour; that's all I ever see of that garden these days.'

Vicky, my third sister, tells that she was with her children and Clara's in the Villanueva Shopping Centre, playing on the little rides. Just before six, she took them to Clara's apartment on Suramericana. When they arrived, Irma, the housekeeper, said: 'Doña Vicky, go to the office, something horrible's happened.' Vicky also knew without being told: 'What happened? Has my father been killed?'

'I left the children screaming and crying, because they had heard, and I went to the office. When I got there they said: "Go quickly, they killed your father." They were crying, hysterical. They told me where he was, up the street. I ran up there. I found hundreds of people there, Clara going crazy. There were lots of bystanders and I saw my father on the ground, with a sheet over him. I couldn't go over to him, I was so shocked I didn't want to see him dead, up close. Later, I always remember the newsreader Pilar Castaño starting her broadcast by saying: "We can't say good evening today, because so many tragic things have happened in the country."' Vicky also remembers the honourable behaviour of Álvaro Uribe Vélez, her ex-boyfriend, who at that time was a senator: she found out that he stopped the session in the Senate, asked for a minute's silence in remembrance of my father, and tabled a motion condemning the crime and sending condolences to our family.

Eva, who moved in the highest circles of Medellín society, was the one with most access to information about those who, in some way, had approved my father's murder. It was she who was told about banana farmers from Urabá, ranchers from the coast, Magdalena Medio landowners allied to Army officers. But she cannot verify everything she was told, and I cannot write it down, since we're not sure it's true, and have no way of proving it.

Sol was doing her internship and got home about six. She found Emma, our beloved life-long housekeeper, crying. She told Sol she'd heard on the radio that Leonardo Betancur had been murdered. 'And your father as well, it seems,' said Emma. Solbia didn't believe her, didn't want to believe her, and locked herself in her room, furious at the atrocious things Emma was saying. The telephone rang and people were saying: 'Good thing they killed that SOB.' Then Sol took a pair of scissors and cut the telephone cord. A while later, looking out the window she saw my father's red car pulling in and thought: 'That Emma is an idiot, telling me my father's been killed, and here he comes.' But when she saw that a chauffer was driving the car, then she did believe it, and burst into tears, overwhelmed with sadness.

That same night I called the director of Public Works, Darío Valencia, who immediately changed our phone number for us, so people wouldn't be able to keep calling to laugh and crow about the murder. We mended the wires that Sol had cut, but of course the phone stayed silent for weeks, because it wasn't only those who wanted to torment us who now didn't have our number, but also those who wanted to offer their condolences or words of solidarity.

After they took his body away, while my sisters and I were in his office on the second floor of my mother's business, we saw a sealed envelope on his desk, addressed to Marta Botero de Leyva, the deputy editor of *El Mundo*. My mother called her, and she came to pick up the envelope, in tears. She opened it: it was his last article: *Where does the violence come from?* it was called, and the newspaper ran it the next day as its editorial. That very afternoon he had written: 'In Medellín there is so much poverty that you can hire a hit man to kill anyone for two thousand pesos. We are living in a time of violence and this violence is born out of inequality. We could have much less violence if the world's riches, including science, technology and morality—these great human creations—were spread more evenly. This is the great challenge we're presented with today, not just us, but humanity as a whole. If the great powers would only allow a united Latin America to look for its own solutions, we'd be much better off. Yes, this is dreaming, but dreaming is a necessary and non-violent precursor to any great triumph. The triumph of bringing about a sane humanity, that one day, over the next ten thousand years, our descendants will see, if we don't self-destruct now or in the near future.'

I write this at La Inés, the farm my father left to us, that my grandfather left to him, that my great-grandfather had left to him, that my great-great-grandfather settled, clearing the bush with his own hands. I draw out these memories from within as one gives birth, as one removes a tumour. I don't look at the screen, I breathe and look outside. It is one of the earth's blessed places. Down below you can see the River Cartama, making its way through the greenery. Above, on the other side, the cliffs of La Oculta and Jericó. The landscape is dotted with trees planted by my father and my grandfather: palm, cedar, orange, teak, mandarin, ackee and mango. I look into the distance and I feel part of this terrain and this landscape. There are flocks of green parrots, blue butterflies, birdsong, the sound of horses' hoofs in the stable, the smell of cow manure in the barn, the occasional dog's bark, cicadas celebrating the heat, ants filing past in lines, each carrying a tiny pink flower. Opposite are the imposing crags of La Pintada that my father taught me to see as the breasts of a naked, reclining woman.

Almost twenty years have passed since he was killed, and during those twenty years, every month, every week, I have felt the inescapable duty, not to avenge his death, but, at least, to tell it. I can't say that his ghost has appeared to me at night, like the ghost of Hamlet's father, to ask me to avenge *his foul and most unnatural murder.* My father always taught us to avoid revenge. The few times I've dreamt of him, in those phantasmal images of memory and fantasy that appear to us as we sleep, our conversations have been more peaceful than anguished, and full of the physical affection we always showed each other. We have not dreamt of each other to ask for revenge, but to embrace.

Perhaps, though, he has said to me, in dreams, like King Hamlet's ghost, 'Remember me,' and I, like his son, can answer: 'Remember thee? Ay, thou poor ghost, while memory holds a seat in this distracted globe. Remember thee? Yea, from the table of my memory I'll wipe away all trivial fond records, all saws of books, all forms, all pressures past, that youth and observation copied there; and thy commandment all alone shall live within the book and volume of my brain, unmix'd with baser matter.'

It is possible that all this will be for nought; no word can bring him back to life, the story of his life and his death will not give new breath to his bones, will not bring back his laughter, or his immense courage, or his persuasive and vigorous words, but in any case I need to tell it. His murderers remain at large; every day they grow in strength; and I cannot fight them with my fists. It is only with my fingers, pressing one key after another, that I can tell the truth and bear witness to the injustice. I use his own weapon: words. What for? For nothing; or for the most simple and essential reason: so it will be known. To extend his memory a little longer, before the inevitable oblivion.

The great Antonio Machado, when Barcelona was about to fall, when the defeat of the Spanish Republic was imminent, wrote the following: 'Valour is a virtue of the unarmed, of the pacifists—never of the thugs— and in the final hour wars are always won by the peace-makers, never by the warmongers. The only brave one is he who can allow himself the luxury of love for his neighbour, a specifically human quality.' That is why I have not written only, or mainly, of the ferocity of those who killed him—the supposed winners of this war— but also of his life dedicated to helping and protecting others.

If to remember, to record, from *cor*, the Latin for heart, means to pass once more through the heart, then I have always remembered him. I have not written of him in all these years for a very simple reason: his memory moved me too much and I was unable to write. The countless times I tried, the words came out damp, dripping with deplorable tears, and I have always preferred to write a drier, more controlled, more distant prose. Now twice ten years have passed and I am able to remain calm as I construct this memorial of grievances. The wound is there, in the place through which memories pass, but now it is a scar more than a wound. I hope I have finally been able to write about my father without an excess of sentimentality, which is always a great risk in writing of this kind. His case is not unique, and perhaps it's not even the saddest. There are thousands and thousands of murdered fathers in this country whose ground is so fertile for death. Nevertheless, I believe my father's case is a special one, and for me it is the saddest, epitomizing the many, many unjust deaths we've suffered here.

I make myself a sad black coffee, put on Brahms' *Requiem*, which blends with the birdsong and the lowing of the cattle. I look for and read a letter my father wrote to me, in January 1984, in reply to a letter of mine in which I told him I wasn't feeling well in Italy, that I was depressed, that I wanted to give up yet another degree and come home. I think I might have even hinted that life itself was weighing heavily on me. His reply came in a letter that has always given me confidence and strength. Copying it out is rather immodest, because in it my father speaks well of me, but at this moment I want to reread it because the letter reveals the unstinting love of a father for his son, that unearned love, which is what helps us, when we've been lucky enough to receive it, to endure the worst things in life, and life itself:

'My darling son: depression at your age is more common than you might think. I remember it very strongly in Minneapolis, Minnesota, when I was about twenty-six and felt like killing myself. I think the winter, the cold, the lack of sunshine, for us tropical creatures, is a trigger. And to tell you the truth, the idea that you might soon unpack your bags here, having chucked in all your European plans, makes your mother and me as happy as could be. You have more than earned the equivalent of any university "degree" and you've used your time so well to educate yourself culturally and personally that if university bores you it's only natural. Whatever you do from here on in, whether you write or don't write, whether you get a degree or not, whether you work in your mother's business, or at *El Mundo*, or at La Inés, or teaching at a high school, or giving lectures like Estanislao Zuleta, or as a psychoanalyst to your parents, sisters and relatives, or simply being Héctor Abad Facio-lince, will be fine. What matters is that you don't stop being what you've been up till now, a *person*, who simply by virtue of being the way you are, not for what you write or don't write, or for being brilliant or prominent, but just for being *the way you are*, has earned the affection, the respect, the acceptance, the trust, the *love*, of the vast majority of those who know you. So we want to keep seeing you in this way, not as a future great author, or journalist or communicator or professor or poet, but as the son, brother, relative, friend, humanist who understands others and does not aspire to be understood. It doesn't matter what people think of you, and gaudy decoration doesn't matter, for those of us who know *who you are*.

'For goodness sake, dear Quinquin, how can you think "we support you" [...] because "that boy could go far"? You've already gone very far, further than all our dreams, better than everything we imagined for any of our children.

'You should know very well that your mother's and my ambitions are not for glory, or for money, or even for happiness, that word that sounds so pretty but is attained so infrequently and for such short intervals (and maybe for that very reason is so valued), for all our children, but that they might at least achieve well-being, that more solid, more durable, more possible, more attainable word. We have often talked of the anguish of Carlos Castro Saavedra, Manuel Mejía Vallejo, Rodrigo Arenas Betancourt and so many quasi-geniuses we know. Or Sábato or Rulfo, or even García Márquez. That doesn't matter. Remember Goethe: "All theory (I would add, *and all art*), dear friend, is grey, but only the golden tree of life springs ever green." What we want is for you to *live*. And living means many better things than being famous, gaining qualifications or winning prizes. I think I too had boundless political ambitions when I was young and that's why I wasn't happy. Only now, when all that has passed, have I felt really happy. And part of that happiness is Cecilia, you, and all my children and grandchildren. Only the memory of Marta Cecilia tarnishes it. I believe things are that simple, after having gone round and round in circles, complicating them so much. We should do away with this love for things as ethereal as fame, glory, success ...

'Well, my Quinquin, now you know what I think of you and your future. There's no need for you to worry. You're doing just fine and you'll do better. Every year will be better, and when you get to my age or your grandfather's age and you can enjoy the scenery around La Inés that I intend to leave to all of you, with the sunshine, heat and lush greenery, you'll see I was right. Don't stay there longer than you feel you can. If you want to come back I'll welcome you with open arms. And if you regret it and want to go back again, we can buy you another *return* flight. As long as you never forget that the most important thing is that you return. A kiss from your father.'

Here I am back in Colombia, writing about him from where he wrote to me, sure that he was right, and that life alone (the green, the warm, the golden) is happiness. Here I am, at La Inés on the plot of land he left to my sisters and me. The miserable murderers who robbed him of his life and us of our happiness and even our sanity for many years, are not going to win, because our love of life and joy (which he taught us) is much stronger than their penchant for death, even though their abominable act left an indelible wound, for as a Colombian poet said, 'what is written in blood cannot be erased.'

In another letter he wrote to me, also from La Inés, in 1986, he said: 'I'm planting other fruit trees besides grapefruit that I hope not just all of you and Daniela will be able to enjoy, but Daniela's children too.' Daniela, my daughter, had just been born that year. A few short weeks before his murder, my father and I held our arms out to her, as she took her very first steps back and forth between us. There is a family chain that has not broken. The murderers have not wiped us out and never will because there is a link of strength and joy here, of love for the land and for life that the murderers could not overcome. Besides, I learned something from my father that the murderers don't know how to do: to use words to express the truth: a truth that will last longer than their lie.

41

At the end of November 1987, three months after they killed my father, on our way out of a ceremony in the Antioquia Assembly, my mother had a strong intuition that someone was going to kill me and shielded me with her body. Two men with backpacks were walking quickly towards us; she stepped in front of me and stood still, staring straight at them. They veered off. I don't know if they meant to do anything, but our blood ran cold. That night, during the ceremony marking the reconstitution of the Antioquia Human Rights Defence Committee, four of us spoke: first the new president, the lawyer, theologian, university professor and member of the Conservative Party, Luis Fernando Vélez. He was a good man, who had published anthropology books on Katío Indian myths. He could neither understand nor tolerate that his colleague from the Teachers' Association, Héctor Abad Gómez had been killed, and wanted to carry on his struggle. I still have a copy of Professor Vélez's speech, which says, at one point: 'The standard-bearers of the honourable undertaking of protecting human rights in Antioquia met martyrdom. Today, in fervent homage to the fallen, the survivors of this first objective are picking up the banner purified by their blood.'

A member of the previous committee, Carlos Gónima, also spoke, as did Gabriel Jaime Santamaría, Communist Party congressman. I spoke as a representative of the family. I didn't want to join the committee and in fact my speech was a declaration of failure. I said, among other things:

'I don't think courage is a quality that is passed down through the genes or, worse, even something that can be taught by example. Nor do I think that optimism is inherited or learned. Proof of this is the person speaking to you, son of a brave and optimistic man, yet full of fear and brimming with pessimism. I am going to speak, then, without encouraging those who want to carry on this battle, which, as far as I'm concerned, is lost.

'You are all here because you have the courage my father had and do not suffer from the feelings of despair and rootlessness that his son does. In you I recognize something I loved and love in my father, something I admire profoundly, but that I have not been able to reproduce in myself and much less to imitate. You have right on your side and so I wish you every success, although my wish cannot be a prediction, however much I'd like it to be. I am here only because I witnessed a good life up close and I want to declare my pain and my rage at the way that life was ripped away from us. Pain without mitigation and rage without expectations. Pain that neither requests nor seeks comfort and rage that does not aspire to vengeance.

'I don't think my defeatist words can have any positive

effect. I speak to you with an inertia that reflects the pessimism of reason as well as the pessimism of action. This is an admission of defeat. It would be futile to tell you that in my family we feel we've lost a battle, as rhetoric demands in cases such as this. Not at all. We feel we've lost the war.

'There is a cliché about our current situation of political violence that needs to be eradicated. This cliché has the persuasive force of an axiom. Few question it; we all receive it passively, unthinkingly, without even discussing the arguments that confirm it or the cracks that might disprove it. This cliché holds that the current political violence we are suffering in Colombia is blind and senseless. But are we experiencing an amorphous, indiscriminate, mad violence? Quite the contrary. Murder is currently being used in a methodical, organized, rational way. More than that, if we sketch an ideological portrait of past victims we can gradually outline the precise features of future victims. And there we might be surprised, perhaps, to see our own faces.'

I have to say that all those who spoke that night except me were killed—Vélez, Santamaría, Gónima. And that the new president who replaced Luis Fernando Vélez on the same committee, Jesús María Valle, was also killed (the paramilitary leader Carlos Castaño also admits to having personally ordered his murder). On 8 December 1987, when Luis Fernando Vélez's corpse turned up in Robledo, I knew I had to leave the country if I didn't want to meet the same fate. Two of my father's best friends were in exile. Carlos Gaviria in Buenos Aires and Alberto Aguirre in Madrid. Another friend who'd left the country in less sordid times, Iván Restrepo, lived in Mexico. I called all three of them from Cartagena, and it was Aguirre who most encouraged me to come to where he was. So I arrived in Madrid, via Panama, on Christmas Day 1987. I had left Medellín on the 18th, without even going home to pack a bag, and hidden in the house of my aunt and uncle and cousins in Cartagena. I remember a friend of one of them, a naval officer, accompanied me to the airport and kept his pistol very visible in his belt until I'd boarded the plane that would take me to Panama to connect with a flight to Madrid the next day. In the early hours of the 25th, Alberto Aguirre was waiting for me in the airport. His hair was long and unkempt, his shirt torn, and he had a woman's pink scarf wrapped around his throat. Carlos Gaviria remained in Buenos Aires in similar conditions. I eventually ended up in Italy, first in Turin and then in Verona, where I began to teach Spanish and to write books. Years later Carlos Gaviria, having returned from Argentina, would help me to publish the first of these, *Malos pensamientos* ('Evil Thoughts'), at the University of Antioquia Press. As if he knew my fragile maturity would still need some fathering, my father had left me these two friends, his best inheritance.

My encounter with Aguirre, in Madrid, was difficult yet also beautiful. He had been in Spain for over three months. Imagine a madman, a madman with long white hair, in a borrowed black overcoat that's too big for him, unshaven, with his shirt torn under the arm, a shadow of dirt on his tanned neck, a hole in the sole of his shoe that lets water in, a woman's pink scarf knotted at his throat. He walks the streets and talks to himself. He talks and talks the way madmen talk, and he looks at girls with burning eyes, for he has no wife and takes consolation in looking. He never crosses a road at a corner, but in the middle of the block. Everyone thinks he's mad; even I thought he was mad when I saw him. It's the end of December, and cold with the dry cold of the high plateau that makes your skin crack like ice. The madman crosses Gran Vía anywhere along it. He stops cars and buses, raising his arms and furiously staring down the drivers, who honk and shout insults, but brake. 'This is called flouting the rules like a *toreador*,' the madman tells me, and it's true, I see with my own eyes how, though he has no cape, he fights the bull cars and red buses of Gran Vía, of La Castellana, not to mention Calle Barquillo or Peñalver.

He goes into a bar, sits down, and the waiters do not serve him. When he sees they're not coming over, he claps his hands, as is customary where he comes from. Since they still don't come, he shouts: 'Hey!' Still they do not serve him. Then he takes off his shoes so they see his worn out socks, rests his feet on the chair in front of him, takes a badly folded newspaper out of his coat pocket, and begins to read, licking his fingers as he turns the pages. After a while, finally, a waiter approaches with that manner they assume when they're going to kick you out, but the madman gives him a withering stare. He orders a *tinto*. When the waiter brings him a glass of red wine, *un vino tinto*, the enraged madman says: 'I ordered a coffee, but you people don't understand Spanish! Bring me a weak black coffee, *un Americano*, as you call it.' This happened over and over again, he tells me, until he decides that from now on he'll only speak English to the waiters. They despise his South American accent, his South American words, his *sudamericana* imprecision, his *sudaca* shoes and, most of all, his obvious *sudaca* poverty. So it's: 'Waiter, please, a coffee, an American coffee, if you don't mind.' Then things go a little better for him, as they consider him an eccentric tourist.

He doesn't always seem like a madman; when he is

freshly showered and has combed his long hair back, he gets mistaken for the poet Rafael Alberti. Sometimes young people come over, in the cafés and bars: 'Señor Alberti, maestro, could you give us your autograph?' And the madman says yes, takes the paper or the serviette they hand him and traces his angular and legible signature: Alberto Aguirre, followed by an exclamation: eat shit! Always the same dedication: ¡Alberto Aguirre, coman mierda! Yes, the madman is mad.

Sometimes he walks down the street weeping. Or not weeping, it's just that he thinks of some detail of his faraway country and his eyes redden with distant visions, the tear ducts get irritated at not seeing and water pours down his cheeks, but he doesn't cry, let's say it rains on him and he lets the rain wet his face, as if it were nothing. And just as salty tears fall from his eyes, sweet words fall from his lips. People think he talks to himself, that the madman talks to himself. But it's not that he talks to himself, actually he's reciting, he recites long verses he knows by heart, by Luis Carlos López, by De Greiff, Spanish romances, whatever springs to mind. He walks the streets of Madrid and recites. Like a madman? No, like an exile.

I repeat: it is late, late at night on 25 December 1987. I had just crossed the Atlantic in an empty plane. That's how I remember it, and it's true: a jumbo jet without passengers, perfectly empty, flying over the Atlantic on Christmas Day 1987. The jet had left Panama City at dusk, the fifteen crew members looking bored as they move around. Pilots, stewardesses, flight attendants, and yours truly. In the middle of the night, the phantom jumbo, two red lights that light up and go out against the dense blackness of the sky, lands in Madrid, and taxis to a gate. There are no visa requirements yet, no queues at immigration; they stamp my passport without looking me in the eye. Years later, when Spain imposed visa restrictions on Colombians, I signed a letter swearing I would not return to Spain. People don't understand why: if visas had been compulsory in 1987 (no one knew me, I didn't have a peso to my name, I couldn't prove anyone was pursuing me), they would never have given me one, not even by mistake, and maybe I wouldn't have been able to leave, as Aguirre had been able to leave, without a visa, to save his neck.

I come out of customs dragging a heavy suitcase, full of old clothes. At the exit is the madman, sitting on a bench beside the door. I stop, look at him, he's grown old in these four months. He's dozing, his chin resting on his chest, his red eyelids pressed tightly closed. He's wearing a threadbare overcoat, a pink scarf, his hair very long, very white, unkempt, several days' growth of beard on his face. He looks like the kind of *clochard* who uses litres of cheap red wine to get to sleep. He doesn't smell of wine. It's him.

I touch his shoulder and he opens his eyes, startled. We look at each other and know the moment is grave. We could burst into tears right there and wail like calves. We swallow hard. An austere embrace, a few mumbled words. 'Good trip?' 'I think so. I slept for most of the way. The plane was empty and I stretched out across the middle seats.' 'Let's get a taxi and go to the pension.' We arrive at the pension. The madman lives with a witch. Long eyeteeth, a missing incisor, bony hands with dirty fingernails that receive my money in advance for ten days of bed, breakfast and siesta. It is almost noon and we go out to walk in the city centre. That's when he shows me how to cross the roads in his style, *a la torera*, and tells me he sometimes passes himself off as Alberti. We laugh and while we laugh I also notice the state of his shoes. Then he tells me why the waiters won't serve him.

Inevitably, we talk about the dead. Yes, they have gone on killing people. Gabriel Jaime Santamaría. Last week Luis Fernando Vélez, the theologian and ethnographer, who had taken up the banner of the Human Rights Defence Committee. A brave man, a martyr, suicidal, all of these. His battered body turned up in Robledo. Inevitably, we talk about 25 August 1987, that dreadful, fateful day when death hit us so close to home, and Aguirre hid, like a rabbit, as he puts it, in an apartment. We haven't seen each other since: four months exactly since we last saw each other. At midday on the 24th, he tells me, he spoke to my father about the list that was going around: both of them sentenced to death. Alberto Aguirre, for being a communist, for writing in defence of trade unions, for fuelling discontent with his newspaper columns. Héctor Abad Gómez, for being the useful idiot of the guerrillas. Something like that. I don't want to repeat the quote verbatim, it makes me feel sick every time I read it.

Aguirre tells me: 'I spoke to him at midday on the Monday and he told me it was serious; that we should try to find someone, see if somehow they could protect us. We were going to see each other on the Wednesday morning at eleven. It wasn't possible.' In hiding, Aguirre wrote his last article: 'There is an exile worse than that beyond borders: the exile of the heart,' it ended by saying. He didn't write for the press again for many years. When he returned, in 1992, he broke his silence with a series of curt, distant reflections on his experience: *On Exile*, they were called, and I published them when I was editor of the University of Antioquia magazine. At the time of writing, I can't find the magazine. On Google, the new library of Babel, there is no trace. These things are being forgotten, although not many years have passed. I have to write them, even if it seems immodest, so that they are not forgotten, or at least so they'll be known for a few more years.

There is something else I want to be known, another story. Let us return to 25 August 1987. That year, so near in my personal history, already seems so long ago in terms of world history: the internet hadn't been invented; the Berlin Wall had not yet fallen; we were still in the death throes of the Cold War; the Palestinian resistance was communist, not Islamist; in Afghanistan the Taliban were allies of the United States against the Soviet invaders. In Colombia, at that time, a terrible witch-hunt had been unleashed: the army and the paramilitaries were murdering members of the *Unión Patriotica*, as well as demobilized guerrillas and, in general, anyone with the slightest whiff of the left or of communism about them.

Carlos Castaño, leader of the AUC (United Self-Defence Forces of Colombia), that murderer who wrote part of Colombia's history using blood for ink and lead for a pen, that murderer who seems to have himself been murdered on the orders of his own brother, said something macabre about this era. He, like all megalomaniacs, had the effrontery to feel proud of his crimes, confessing unashamedly in a filthy book: 'I devoted myself to blowing out the brains of those who were really acting as urban subversives. I don't regret that and I never will! For me that determination was wise. I executed fewer people by taking the right aim. They would have kept the war going on longer. I'm convinced that I'm the one who is now bringing the war to its end. If God has illuminated me, it is above all to understand this.'

This visionary, who in his wisdom ended our war (which is still going on) twenty years ago, later describes how they decided who should be executed: 'That's where the Group of Six comes in. The Group of Six came from a long line of national history, men from the highest echelons of Colombian society. The crème de la crème! I met the first of them in 1987, days after the death of Jaime Pardo Leal. [...] They would be shown a list of enemies' names, jobs or whereabouts. "Which ones should be executed?" I'd ask and they would take the piece of paper into another room. They'd come back with the name or names of the people that should be executed indicated, and the action was carried out with very good results. [...] They were true nationalists who never invited me to eliminate people without good reason. They taught me to love and believe in Colombia.' Then he confessed that he had killed Pedro Luis Valencia, a week before my father was killed, with help from the State intelligence services; later he admitted that he killed Luis Felipe Vélez, in the same place and on the same day my father was killed.

I'm not going to sully my fingers quoting this patriot any further. But let's return to 1987 and that pool of blood produced by him and his accomplices. To the corner of Calle Argentina and Carrera Girardot, in Medellín. A pool of blood and a body lying face up, covered with a sheet, like the Manet painting, I don't know if you've seen it, but if you do see it one day you'll remember. I am kneeling at the edge of that pool of blood. When that blood poured out, as the assassin said, a mind was obliterated. 'Blow their brains out,' is the phrase the murderers use to mean kill them. And it's quite true, that's what it's about, extinguishing intelligence. I am sitting there and a desperate, white-haired, white-bearded man runs up to us like a madman. A man who never acts like a madman, a serene, balanced, rational man. He arrives, and it's at this moment I tell him, beg him: 'Carlos, get lost, go and hide. You have to leave; if you don't they'll kill you too and we don't want any more deaths!' He had been going to go with my father and Leonardo to the murdered teacher's wake, but he didn't get there on time because his dentist (and mine, and my father's) was running late, and he had to wait for his appointment. That's how he was saved.

We speak for a moment, between tears and impotent rage. After a while he leaves the scene, but not yet the country. The next day, at the funeral, with shaking hands but a very firm voice, he is able to read a speech. He has guessed it all, without being able to know the precise details: this is an act of ordinary fascism that we are facing. 'Héctor Abad Gómez's attachment to the highly humanist idea of the liberal creed had made him flexible and tolerant when in Colombia there is no longer any room for anyone but fanatics.' Finally he recalls the disgusting words of Millán Astray, and repeats them, these words that are, he is sure, the assassins' slogan: 'Long live death! Down with intelligence!' It's the same as Castaño's idea: you kill in order to obliterate the mind.

A few months later, this same very white-haired, white-bearded man is walking down Avenida de Mayo and stops at number 829. He's wearing a dark suit and tie, and carries a book under his arm. The door with this number is that of a café, perhaps the most beautiful in Buenos Aires, the Tortoni. The waiters do not hesitate but come straight over to take his order, for this dignified gentleman is the very image of decorum. He orders a dry, red vermouth, and some sparkling mineral water. No one asks for his autograph. He opens his book and reads and underlines and carefully notes down his observations. It is one of Plato's dialogues. I can't quite make out which one, but let's suppose it's *Lysis*, the one on friendship, in which there is, curiously, a discussion about white hair: 'Suppose, says Socrates, that someone should rub white lead over your blond locks. Would they then be truly white, or simply appear so?'

Frankly I don't understand what Socrates is saying in that dialogue. They are talking about friendship, about good and evil, about someone who does not dye his white hair to disguise it, but instead dyes his hair white, so that he looks white-haired, when in fact he's not. Whenever I try to read Plato's dialogues I get muddled. I need a white-haired professor like this one I'm telling you about, who doesn't dye his blond hair white, or his white hair black, but whose hair turned white in his youth, prematurely, like the madman in Madrid.

White hair is associated with old age, but also with serenity and wisdom. The gentleman in the Café Tortoni is another Colombian exile, with very white hair, who came back years later and has been responsible for passing some sentences and laws that, even now, give us a little hope that this country of ours is not completely barbarous. Carlos Gaviria is one of the few people with an independent and liberal mind, when there are again fears that in Colombia the darkness that triumphed at the end of the 1980s could return. I didn't see him in Buenos Aires, in those years, but we wrote to each other often and when I went to Argentina for the first time, not long ago, he recounted his daily itinerary, the streets and cafés where he spent the days of his exile; parks, walks around Borges' neighbourhood, new and second-hand bookshops.

I have no doubt that there are still some people today

who wish to obliterate the minds of people like Alberto Aguirre and Carlos Gaviria, two Colombians who were forced into exile, who saved their own lives and came back, to carry on here, as the most important and free moral conscience we have. It was not long ago, in 1987, that all this happened. Some did have their brains blown out. But some saved their necks by going into exile, to Spain or Argentina or other places, and have now come back, as white-haired as they were then, even wiser than before. I'm greyer every day myself, although not like them. But I do hope to be worthy of each one of my white hairs. Carlos and Alberto are two great friends I inherited from my greatest friend, that other mind, who did not manage to escape into exile and was obliterated by the bloody hands of the assassins.

OBLIVION

42

We are all condemned to dust and to oblivion, and the people I've evoked in this book are either dead or about to die or at best they will die—I mean, we will die—in a number of years that can't be counted in centuries but in decades. *'Yesterday's gone, tomorrow has yet to arrive / today's slipping away without stopping at all; / I am a was, and a will be, and a tired is ...'* said Quevedo, referring to our fleeting existence, always heading inevitably towards the moment when we'll cease to be. We survive for a few fragile years, still, after death, in the memory of others, but this personal memory, with every moment that passes, also comes ever closer to disappearing. A book is a simulacrum of remembering, an *aide-mémoire*, a desperate attempt to make a little more lasting what is irremediably finite. All these people with whom the most intimate weft of my memory is woven, all those presences that were my childhood and my youth, are either gone, and are only phantoms, or are on their way to disappearing, as am I, and we are all future spectres who still move about on the earth. In short, all these people of flesh and blood, all these friends and relatives I love so much, all those enemies who hate me so devotedly, will be no more real than fictional characters, at best ghostly evocations and spectres, though nothing more than a handful of dust will be left of most of them, and an inscription on a tombstone whose letters will gradually fade away in the cemetery. The time of living memory is so short, if we see it in perspective, that a wise man understands that, 'already we are the oblivion we shall be,' as Borges said. For him this oblivion and that elemental dust we will become were consolations 'beneath the blue indifference of heaven.' If heaven, as it seems, is indifferent to all our joys and all our misfortunes, if the universe could not care less whether mankind exists or not, going back to being the nothing we came from is the worst misfortune, yes, but at the same time, is also the greatest relief and only rest, for we will no longer suffer the tragedy that is the awareness of the pain and death of the people we love. Although I must believe it, I don't want to imagine the painful moment when the people I most love—my children, my friends and relatives—also stop existing, which will be the moment when I too will stop living, as someone's vivid memory, forever. My father didn't know either, didn't want to know, when I would die. What he did know, and this, perhaps, is another of our fragile consolations, is that I would remember him forever, and that I would fight to rescue him from oblivion for at least a few years more, I don't know how many, with the evocative power of words. If words transmit part of our ideas, our memories, our thoughts—and we have yet to find a better vehicle, so that there are still those who confuse language and thought—if words trace an approximate map of our mind, I have transferred a good part of my memory to this book, and since all men are brothers, in a certain sense, because what we think and say is similar, because our ways of feeling are almost identical, I hope to have in you, readers, some allies, some accomplices, able to strike the same chords in that dark soundbox of the soul, so similar in us all, that is the mind shared by our species. 'O let the soul her slumbers break!' begins one of the greatest of Spanish poems, which is the first inspiration for this book, because it is also a homage to the memory and to the life of an exemplary father. What I was looking for was this: that my deepest memories would awaken. And if my memories enter into harmony with some of yours, and if what I've felt (and will stop feeling) is understandable and identifiable with something that you feel or have felt, then forgotten as we shall be, in the fleeting spark of your neurons, thanks to the eyes, many or few, that might briefly pause over these words, the oblivion that awaits can be deferred a moment more.

1 Héctor with his parents on the day of his circumcision
2 Héctor with his father at Bahía Solano, a few
   months before his father died
3 Héctor Abad's father with Héctor's sisters, reading
4 Héctor's father with Riki, one of the grandchildren

On the Design

As book design is an integral part of the reading experience, we would like to acknowledge the work of those who shaped the form in which the story is housed.

Tessa van der Waals (Netherlands) is responsible for the cover design, cover typography, and art direction of all World Editions books. She works in the internationally renowned tradition of Dutch Design. Her bright and powerful visual aesthetic maintains a harmony between image and typography and captures the unique atmosphere of each book. She works closely with internationally celebrated photographers, artists, and letter designers. Her work has frequently been awarded prizes for Best Dutch Book Design.

The font used on the cover is Cheap Pine from Hannes van Döhren of HvD Fonts, Berlin. Cheap Pine is a roughly drawn, condensed font and has a printed hand-made appearance. The font is a tribute to the wood type of the eighteenth century and nineteenth century. The image of the shadow of a palm tree in the background is one of the graphic designer's own.

The cover has been edited by lithographer Bert van der Horst of BFC Graphics (Netherlands).

Suzan Beijer (Netherlands) is responsible for the typography and careful interior book design of all World Editions titles.

The text on the inside covers and the press quotes are set in Circular, designed by Laurenz Brunner (Switzerland) and published by Swiss type foundry Lineto.

All World Editions books are set in the typeface Dolly, specifically designed for book typography. Dolly creates a warm page image perfect for an enjoyable reading experience. This typeface is designed by Underware, a European collective formed by Bas Jacobs (Netherlands), Akiem Helmling (Germany), and Sami Kortemäki (Finland). Underware are also the creators of the World Editions logo, which meets the design requirement that 'a strong shape can always be drawn with a toe in the sand.'